AF797476

The Legal Felony

The Legal Felony

QUASI-JUDICIAL IMMUNITY IS BACK WINDOWS FOR COMMITTING CRIMES

◆ ◆ ◆

Abdelbaset Youssef, M.D.

The Author claims responsibility of truth of all of the contents of this book and assumes all liabilities, further states that documents related to the facts of this book are in the subject Federal and State Courts' records, Michigan Attorney General, and other agencies. The Author considers this book his self-defense, and it is in his patients and general public interest.

P. O Box 478, Dearborn Heights, Michigan 48127
astoria.medical@yahoo.com
www.jesusfromindiatojapan.com
ISBN-13: 9780692999295
ISBN-10: 0692999299
Library of Congress Control Number: 2018900879
Abdelbaset Youssef, Inkster, MI

Printed and distributed by www.CreateSpace.com

To my Patients

One day, I was absent from my office for two weeks, some of my patients asked me if I had planned for them if something happened to me. At that time it had not come to our mind that there were causes other than death and diseases could deprive us of seeing each other. I wrote this book so they may know that I had not betrayed them.

About the Author

◆ ◆ ◆

Abdelbaset Youssef, MD, author of Jesus: From India to Japan, is Egyptian Physician had worked for seven years as a dermatologist at King Faisal Hospital Makah, Saudi Arabia before he immigrated to the United States of America, which granted him political asylum. In New York, he was trained and certified by the American Board of Internal Medicine. Currently, he is US citizen internist. He has been interested in reading about Laws and Politics. He fled from the Middle East for better legal and political environment to find the United States Legal System disappointing. He lives with his wife in Bloomfield Hills, Michigan, has two sons physicians and one daughter medical student.

Contents

Abbreviations

◆ ◆ ◆

LARA: Department of Licensing and Regulatory Affairs
Mr. Schuette: Bill Schuette, Michigan Attorney General
ALJ: Administrative Law Judge
PFD: ALJ's Proposal for Decision
Exceptions: Opposition to Proposal for Decision
Mr. Hudson: Andrew Hudson, Assistant Attorney General
Jessica Taub: Jessica Taub, Assistant Attorney General
AAG Assistant Attorney General
Mr. Regan: Robert Regan, R. Ph., Investigator in LARA
Dr. Hopper: John Hopper, M.D., Expert Witness in LARA
Dr. Szymanski: Dennis Szymanski, M.D., Board of Medicine FDA
Food and Drug Administration

Introduction

◆ ◆ ◆

THE TERM FELONY, IN SOME common law countries, means a serious crime. The word originates from English common law where felonies were originally crimes that involved confiscation of a convicted person's land and goods. Other crimes were called misdemeanors. Felony is a crime punishable by minimum one year in prison.

The felonies are classified by violent or nonviolent, according to its seriousness, and by subject matter.

Crimes against justice, such as malfeasance in office, miscarriage of justice, obstruction of justice, filing false documents, fraud, perverting the course of justice and perjury are examples of felonies about legal proceedings.

Discrimination in hiring for job or housing is a crime, but it is legal if it was done against the felon so it is a legal crime. The Federal Court and the State Court decided that due to the absolute quasi-judicial immunity, we cannot sue state officials and employees for crimes against justice such as perjury and obstruction of justice if they did these acts about a quasi-judicial proceeding such as physician disciplinary proceeding. Honorable Michael Talbot, Chief Judge, the Michigan Court of Appeals asserted that ("falsity or malice on the part of the witness does not abrogate the privilege"). My understanding, since law protects these crimes, they can be called legal felonies.

I am not resisting the court judgments seeking to change them, or claiming the judges got them wrong. Judges are restricted by the law whatever it is perfect or biased. I am presenting my opinion that absolute quasi-judicial immunity is double edge weapon violate some people's civil rights. Some officials acting above the law can select specific people for illegal injury under the haven of this legal doctrine and make victims, who need to be redressed, unprotected, and deprived of their constitutional rights.

This book is to address what I consider two major defects in the United States legal system. The flaws should not be in a state claiming leadership of the free and democratic worlds as they violate the Constitution and human rights.

The Statue of Liberty is not aware of what is going on in its backyard because it is busy looking east to the old world.

Absolute judicial immunity (immunity of the judges) was extended to the officials and employees of the State's government and its agencies to be absolute quasi-judicial immunity.

The United States Constitution Amendment XIV says: "nor shall any State deprive any person of life, liberty, or property, without due process of law; nor deny to any person within its jurisdiction the equal protection of the laws."

Now, this is not true anymore. The State officials can deprive any person of life, liberty, or property, without due process of law and they can commit many kinds of felonies on the nose of the Constitution and the nose of the court, once they do their crimes about executive quasi-legal proceedings such as physician disciplinary proceeding.

Due to the absolute quasi-judicial immunity, both the Federal and State Courts decided that we cannot sue the State officials or employees for damage or injury resulting from wrong acts were done about quasi-legal executive proceedings even the actions were done intentionally false or in malice for inflicting unnecessary damage or injury.

State officials can use this legal doctrine as a back window to commit crimes against any person they have access to his interest.

Absolute quasi-judicial immunity of the State officials created sect of noble people above the Constitutions and laws; state officials call it higher level. They are armed by the Office of the State Attorney General. This legal doctrine makes over protected community similar to the Church in the middle ages in Europe or the communist parties.

They line up with each other to defend their interests and corruptions illegally. If anyone of the general public injured or just touched anyone from the State community or related to any one of them, his life would be ruined. I was not the first one or the last one to be my life destroyed and thousands of my patients injured and suffered for nonsense reasons. Hundreds of physicians have been injured by nonsense complaints and felonies of obstruction of justice under the haven of the absolute quasi-judicial immunity.

I am presenting two similar cases where the state officials lined up against a person for touching interest of one of them.

I am a physician, had been practicing medicine for more than 30 years, the last ten years I dedicated my work for treating patients who have chronic pain syndrome along with the other medical problems and addiction. A retired nurse complained that I was giving her son narcotic while he was able to control his pain by Motrin. FDA does not approve Motrin for treating chronic pain syndrome resulted from construction work accident and MRI documented herniated disc and spinal stenosis and radiculopathy. The lady is a cousin of an administrative law judge (ALJ). The ALJ works at Licensing and Regulatory Affairs, {LARA},

Mr. Andrew Hudson, Assistant Attorney General, works at LARA as well. Mr. Hudson filed a complaint against me and further stated that in 2009, I gave patient C.H. combined medicine contained Acetaminophen 750 mg while she was taking the combined medication contained Acetaminophen 500 mg from another doctor before she came to my office. He was not aware that Acetaminophen is not narcotic; it is Tylenol which is available for sale at the gas station. The complaint had not had any smell of medicine. Addressing the defects of the complaint created personal conflict with Mr. Hudson. Later in a hearing, he stated that he made mistakes because the complaint was outside his experience. After I refused to pay $5000 fine because of no reason for fine, Mr. Hudson scheduled a hearing and selected the same administrative law judge {ALJ}, cousin of the complainant to conduct the hearing. Mr. Hudson brought other state employees, who had committed a grave, naked perjury under oath about my management of the ALJ's relative. During the proceedings, I have been victimized by more than 17 naked legally protected felonies. My medical license was suspended, first for six months and then they stated in an official document (PFD), what means that because I appealed the 6-month suspension the suspension should be extended for years. I lost my practice and thousands of patients mostly disable and stable in my office for about ten years were injured and exposed to a risk of death. The Law *MCL 333.16204(c)* says it is very difficult for these kinds of patients to secure their treatments; moreover, they were prejudiced when they went to other providers because they were coming from a doctor, sanctioned for drug-related issues. Both Federal and State Courts decided that I could not sue them for injury resulted from their acts even if the actions were false or in malice because absolute quasi-judicial immunity shields them. Moreover, the courts could not enjoin their prospective continuous violations.

Another case similar to my case; Dr. Bruce Serven, Chiropractic, examined a post-car accident patient, who was referred to him by State Farm Insurance Company to see if he needed chiropractic work. Dr. Serven discovered that patient A.E. did not need this kind of treatment. The insurance company stopped paying for Health Quest of Burton Chiropractic, PC.

Dr. Solomon Cogan was the co-owner of Health Quest, and he was the Chairman of Michigan Board of Chiropractic. Dr. Serven alleged that Dr. Cogan threatened him, "Obviously I need to see you on a higher level." The assistant attorney general filed a complaint against Dr. Serven, and through quasi-judicial executive proceeding Dr. Serven was punished for one-year probation, later the Michigan Court of Appeals found it was illegal punishment and reversed it. Dr. Serven filed a complaint about damage in the circuit court, which denied Dr. Cogan and the other state officials' motion for summary dismiss. The Court of Appeals dismissed the case in favor of Dr. Cogan and the other state officials for they were shielded by the absolute quasi-judicial immunity against suing for the subject wrong acts.

Another defect in the legal system is hypocrisies in the legislature. This means when we read the legislature we find it okay but in practice, it turns to be different. An example; MCL 333.16228, requires the Board of Medicine establishes controlled prescriptions panel of 10 physicians to review controlled medicine complaint before its filing. In real life, I received a complaint was not reviewed by even a nurse.

The Court of Appeals stated that establishing the ten physician panel is optional to the Board of Medicine and there is no law requires a specific person to write or review the complaint. The general public and people worldwide, who read the legislature, believe all of the complaints about controlled medicine were reviewed by ten physician panel, which gives the complaints false credibility.

Order of suspension my license for six months subject of judicial review, when I filed the appeal in the court, Mr. Hudson failed to stay the enforcement of the order for pending appeal. The suspension was for six months, and it was extended to be for years as retaliation for filing appeal, while the appeal took 18 months.

The hypocrisy is giving the decision of staying enforcement of the order and extending it in the hand of the person who issued it in the same time, the appeal takes 18 months, and there was no mechanism for protection against retaliation.

During the pendency of the appeal, Mr. Hudson, Jessica Taub, and the ALJ issued PFD stating on an official document that means that because I filed the appeal, the suspension should be extended to be for years. The Court of Appeals had not had jurisdiction over the new order that extends and supersedes the pending order, so the appeal was hijacked before it was decided.

No one can say the judicial review other than a big hoax or deep hole. The appeal changed the suspension from 6 months to be for good. The general public and people, who read the legislature, believe the victim has ample chance for judicial review while it was just a deep hole.

I waited 18 months to hear from the appeal. The Court of Appeals stated that it is not its role to assess the credibility of the witness or documents or even validity of the hearing or review.

MCL 333.16237(3) In reviewing the recommended findings of fact and conclusions of law of the hearings examiner and the record of the hearing, a disciplinary subcommittee may request the hearings examiner to take additional testimony or evidence on a specific issue or may revise the recommended findings of fact and conclusions of law as determined necessary by the disciplinary subcommittee, or both.

The Court of Appeals stated that once is stated in the order that the record was reviewed satisfy the requirements of the legislature. Just saying it was reviewed impossible to replace the real review as described by law and address my oppositions to Proposal for Decision and my evidence for they committed perjury. Again; general public believes the opposition to the PFD was indeed reviewed and addressed by the Board of Medicine in detail as described in the legislature, which was not true.

My attorney blamed me. He stated I should not respond to the complaint or argue. I should do like all other physicians, just say I was sorry I would not do it again and bow to them so that they would be easy on me. I should not try taking my rights by law. I should be submissive to stay safe.

The documents carry the name of the Board of Medicine, while, according to my knowledge, the members of the Board are very busy physicians travel to Lansing Michigan every two months for few hour meeting as guests for coffee and voting on the orders. Their membership is just honor for their excellence in medicine. The business of the Board is run by young assistant attorney generals; who do everything. All of Michigan physicians are in their left hands.

In 1982, Egypt improved the Emergency Law. The new law allows the officer may arrest any person, but the victim can challenge the arrest in the court, which shall issue the final order within 45 days.

Everybody in Egypt or worldwide knows the maximum period of an illegal arrest is 45 days. Only the victims, who were arrested for up to or more than ten years, know that the law did not set the maximum number of illegal arrests.

What I could not imagine was to see the same legal hypocrisies in the United States legal system.

If I had known that the State officials and employees were immune against suing for wrongful acts, the judicial review had a short arm, and the legislature practice was not the same as it is read, I would submissively pay the $5000 fine and save myself and my patients from such devastating damages and suffering. Every American needs to read this book, so he may not fell into the deep hole as I did.

CHAPTER 1

On the way to America

◆ ◆ ◆

SADDAM HUSAIN, THE PREVIOUS PRESIDENT of Iraq, after he lost the 8-year war with Iran, decided to make Iraq a great country like France and UK. He needed power and money so he started to develop nuclear weapon program and tried to take Kuwait, Eastern Saudi Arabia, Qatar, and UAE so that he might control more than 70% of the World's oil and put the tag price of the oil and gas.

In 1990, Saddam asked the US ambassador in Bagdad about what America would do if he took Kuwait; she said that the USA has no joint defense agreement with Kuwait, which Saddam considered green light. The US had noticed the Saddam's army moving toward Kuwait, and then they told Kuwait authority that they could stop Saddam if Kuwait let them did. Kuwait authority was confused, whether Saddam or America wanted to take them. Kuwait authority called the Egyptian president, Hosni Mubarak, about what they could do. Mubarak fled to Iraq, where Saddam told him, it was impossible to think this way.

Kuwait authority believed Mubarak so that they did not allow Americans parked their stuff in Kuwait and in the same time they believed America, so all of the princes and the VIPs took their valuables and fled overnight to Saudi Arabia. At early morning Saddam had jumped on Kuwait. Car dealers distributed their cars free to the foreign workers, who had entered Kuwaiti houses and filled their pockets with gold, jewelry, Kuwaiti money and much more. Kuwait became the 20th Iraqi Province. Saddam started to move toward Saudi Arabia.

Saudi spoiled boys were not ready to defend their country. Egypt took the side of Kuwait and Saudi Arabia while the other Arab Countries divided between Iraq and Saudi Arabia. Mubarak felt severe pain for Saddam promised him he would not invade Kuwait but he did on the same night. Mubarak said to Saddam, on a TV speech; you stabbed me in the back! The USA and 45 other countries rushed to form a huge army in the Saudi Arabian desert, in a war operation called the Desert Storm. Osama Bin-Laden retuned from Afghanistan after they conquered the Soviet Union and opposed the King in dependence on foreigners for defense.

Vatican Pope blamed the western countries for defending Saudi Arabia, which did not allow building Churches. The Saudi King, Fahd responded on the TV that he just overnight prayed help from Almighty God and then in the next morning he received calls from almost every country in the world, ready to send troops. Finally, they made temporary tent Churches in the land of war for the Christian soldiers.

In 1990, while they had been preparing for the war, I was a dermatologist in my private practice in Jirga, Egypt, a small city 350 miles south of Cairo. Many foreign workers including physicians had left Saudi Arabia. I decided; it would be good if I went to Saudi Arabia for few months to work, visit the Holy Land and watch the war actions by direct vision. My friends warned me about the risks of the war; I stated that the war would be between the Iraqi army, which was tired from 8-year war with Iran against 46 very advanced armies. The war would not take more than few hours.

Saddam stated that president Nasser of Egypt, in 1956, fought UK, France, and Israel and lost the war but he emerged as a hero, so he wanted to take footsteps of Nasser. In 1956, Nasser nationalized the Suez Canal then Egypt was attacked by UK, France, and Israel. They destroyed the Egyptian Army but they lost the war and, due to international pressure, they withdrew from Egypt. Since then the UK and France were downgraded to be second degree great countries and left first degree spots to the USA and the Soviet Union. Nasser had emerged as one of the World's leaders. Saddam goal was losing the war and gaining the historical name of the leader who fought 46 armies. For this reason, I believed the war would happen anyway.

On 12/4/1990, I had visited the grand mosque in Makah, before I took the bus for Riyadh. I had received my work as a dermatologist in a multispecialty clinic. The majority of people had left Riyadh for living in Makah. Qur'an stated in many verses that almighty God, more than 4000 years ago, had promised Prophet Abraham that Makah would be safe secure and vibrant forever. Because the City of Makah could not accommodate all Saudi people, people were living in the desert.

The war started by 2500 planes destroyed almost all of the Iraqi army in few hours, except for some Iraqi jet fighters fled to Iran where they were confiscated. It took about one month to hunt the stray soldiers in the Iraqi desert and USA used B52 strategic bombers for the soldiers inside underground bonkers. I read from one source that Iraq in addition to devastating nationwide damages they lost a huge number of soldiers in this war. Saddam considered it a victory as he got his goal of fighting 46 armies.

During the month of the war, we had been watching from the roof of our house the panorama of the surface to surface Iraqi Scud missiles and US Patriot anti-missiles in the sky of Riyadh. Patriot system failed to oppose only two Scuds; one destroyed vacant high rise building in downtown Riyadh, where just one person died, and the other one destroyed swimming pool in a university close to the main airport.

I noticed, the physicians who were certified by the American Board of Dermatology was paid very high salary, the cost of living was very low, and there was no Tax. I called the US education advisor in the US Embassy, whether it was possible to be certified by the American Board of Dermatology. She told me sure; just call the Chairman of the American Board of Dermatology to send the exam to her office in the US Embassy. She gave me his name and his address at Henry Ford Hospital in Detroit. The Board Chairman told me I had to pass the United States Medical Licensing Examination {USMLE} parts I and II exams and I had to finish four years residency training in an accredited dermatology program in the USA before taking the Dermatology Board Exam.

I moved to work as a Specialist Dermatology at King Faisal Hospital Makah, Saudi Arabia.

Talking about politics for Saudis and non-Saudis was a criminal act. In the Hospital, we used to discuss politics in closed rooms. Every physician spoke about the political pain in his country. A Syrian doctor compared the selection of presidents in Syria and Egypt. In Egypt, no need for everybody to go, in the day of the election, to say yes or no for the president's period renewal for further terms. The governmental election centers were doing the job for the people, and the president used to get 100% attendance and 99% approval rate, while in Syria everybody should go and say yes. One Syrian physician had failed to go in the day of the election so he had to escape to Jordon for good so that he would not pay his life as a price for his neglect of election duty.

In Syria, the election room has a screen, the person has the option to hide behind the screen and write yes or no in secret, but nobody had been going behind the screen because this was evidence that he did a bad job and put his life in risk. Everybody should go and say yes without going behind the screen. The attendance was 100%, and approval rate was 100% in visually seen as a very clean election procedure. We considered that the political condition in Egypt was better than its condition in Syria. Egyptians should be thankful for their government for it, unlike Syrian government, was doing their election duties, without going personally to say yes as in Syria.

In Saudi Arabia, there is no such kind of election's headache. The Saudi regime is old kinghood type of government. The King is the official owner of everything in the country. For example, when the government distributes pieces of land they say it is a gift from the King. No one is allowed to discuss politics. Saudi people did not know what was going on in their country. Many Saudis believed that the presence of USA's army in their land was an occupation and the royal family sold their country to the US for staying the crown. A Saudi physician told me that in the past every nation was occupied except Saudi Arabia, now the only occupied country is Saudi Arabia, we had to pay the same price that the other countries' people paid for their independence.

I passed the United States Medical Licensing Examination {USMLE} parts I and II but it took a long time to pass English test called TOEFL with the required score. After I had become ready to go to America, I had a massive heart attack, and I survived cardiac arrest. I had been enjoying excellent health. One day I slept after I had heavy fatty dinner I woke up on an early morning with severe chest pain. I drove few blocks to the Hospital, where I had been working, and then I woke up after four-day coma. Even though I had needed heart workup, I started preparing for traveling to America. I did not know anything about anything in America. I heard from friends many stories of failure. An Egyptian pediatrician told me that his brother who was a pharmacist immigrated along with his family to Canada. He could not work as a pharmacist, and his work in a flower shop was not enough to pay his apartment rent, so he returned to his private pharmacy in Cairo. One Saudi physician just came from New York told me that he watched a crime in the street. American violence movies give a false idea about the security condition.

I left my job at King Faisal Hospital in the Holy City and sent my wife and three children to Egypt, and I took Saudi flight to New York. I had a feeling of fear mixed with hope and happiness for the unknown dream for my family and me. I had heart disease I did not know if I would survive to see my wife and children again. I slept on the airplane on my way to New York, and I saw a dream that I was swimming in the sea and my two boys had been swimming one behind the other beside me. I interpreted the vision, in the hope it comes true as I would see my children and they would take footsteps in my career which came true. I felt as if I was, the 15th century, Christopher Columbus sailing to discover the Americas. From JFK airport I started the new adventure.

I had two weeks reservation in YMCA, Main Street, Flushing New York. Flushing, NY is China Town, people speak only Chinese. I went to get some food. In a store, I asked if I had one kilogram of apple. I couldn't understand the store agent who spoke only Chinese. It did not come to my mind that American spoke other than English, so I believed he spoke English. I repeated trial in many stores; I asked myself where was my English and how I could live without practical English. Some sellers understood my English, but they did not understand word kilogram as the only pound is used in the USA as weight measure unit. I saw the signs were saying LB; I asked him if he might give me one LB, he did not know what LB was. I did not understand what LB stood for as well.

At night, in the hotel, I heard heavy gun shooting; my mind went back to the violent movies and asked myself, how many people were killed this night. Next day I saw building next to the hotel with a sign saying {Police Training Center}.

It took two weeks looking for a room for rent, until I found an Egyptian, from whom I rented a room in his apartment in Astoria, NY. I kept the name of Astoria with me in Michigan, so I named my medical office in Michigan; Astoria Medical P C. I started to fill applications for Dermatology Residency Programs. I filed 100 applications to all of the 100 Dermatology Programs. Preparing one application takes a long time. Application to residency programs is seasonal; it means if I could not get chance that year, I had to wait for the next year. Over two years, I failed to get a position in a Dermatology Program. Dermatology Programs offer about only 300 positions every year to be filled from more than 150 Medical Schools in the USA. Dermatology is attractive specialty so practically there was no spot for the Foreign Medical Graduates. I had to give up looking for Dermatology as a profession. Internal Medicine was the next choice.

CHAPTER 2

Jamaica Hospital Hundred Percent Pass Pate

◆ ◆ ◆

AT THAT TIME, RESIDENCY PROGRAMS of all specialties needed about 20,000 physicians. US Medical Schools graduates were approximately 15,000, so 5000 spots were available for the Foreign Medical Graduates. Nearly 30,000 foreign medical graduates were competing for these 5000 spots. US Medical Schools were able to graduate 20,000 but the policy was to keep the door open for selected applicants from world-wide, some of them could have extraordinary ability. This policy is not for medicine only but all sciences. This policy is good for the USA, the foreigner, and his country. An example; the Egyptian Ahmed Zewail, he was given a chance to get Ph.D., in Chemistry, he got Nobel Prize from Caltech University in California. If he stayed in Egypt, he would be a school teacher.

Foreign Medical Graduate, after he finishes his residency training, he has to leave for his country of origin, except for if he served at least five years practicing medicine in medically underserved areas such as prisons, rural areas and downtown poor populations, which American graduates dislike to work there.

I had been accepted to Jamaica Hospital Medical Center, Jamaica, New York for three years training in the Internal Medicine Residency

Program. Once I had a contract with Jamaica Hospital, I called my family for living with me in the USA.

Residency Programs compete for excellence. The measurement is the percentage pass rate of the first time board exam takers, graduates of that program, who pass the Board Exam. 100 % Board Exam pass rate was the target, and then the competition was for which program could get 100 percent rate for successive years. No hospital got 100 percent rate for more than five consecutive years. Even the top hospitals such as Mayo Clinic or John Hopkins, it was difficult for them to get 100 percent in one year. The top hospitals have the power to compete; they select the top graduates, less load of work and excellent teaching programs. Hospitals like Jamaica Hospital, how it could compete with Mayo Clinic and win the race? Jamaica Hospital was not attractive for exceptional graduates, the workload was more than double of the maximum permitted by law, and they did not have good teaching program.

The Chairman of the Internal Medicine Program at Jamaica Hospital, who got 100 percent pass rate for five successive years, was looking for six years to be the only one in America. He had been selecting foreign medical graduates with the highest scores in USMLE. He used to take about 19 residents for the first year and then, put them in competition, and the next years, he had been removing the residents with the lowest grades in the monthly exams. The remaining 13 residents would pass the Board exam very easily. The resident who was removed from the program could not get a position in other programs. The Hospital could not remove American graduates by this illegal way as they were legally supported. Foreign medical graduate, who was removed either returned to his country or found a non-medical job.

Santucci, M.D., a retired cardiologist and Chairman of the Department of Internal Medicine in Jamaica Hospital. He achieved 100 percent pass rate for his residents' internal medicine board exam in 5 successive years. His dream was getting 100 percent pass rate in more than five successive years so that he would be the first nationwide. Jamaica Hospital is a private hospital in medically underserved areas and poor neighborhoods. Resident physicians had been working more than the double of the maximum load allowed by the Accreditation Council for Graduate Medical Education (ACGME) in the same time they had to compete against each other to survive removal from the Program. Jamaica Hospital's internal medicine program was not attractive for the American school graduates; moreover, if they got American graduates they would have the lowest scores in the United States Medical Licensing Examination {USMLE} so that Jamaica was not interested in them as well.

Jamaica Hospital, to compete with the top programs such as Mayo clinic and win the race should depend on the foreign medical graduates with scores exceed the Americans' scores and apply the policy of illegal selective removal of the residents. Mayo Clinic and the other top programs could not score like Jamaica in the matter of the Board pass rate.

Through the National Residents Matching Program (NRMP), Jamaica Hospital had given me a contract for three years training program in internal medicine leading to sitting for the American Board of Internal Medicine exam. I called my family to the USA for pending start of a stable job and hoped that I would have insurance to do angioplasty for my heart.

During the pre-employment exam, while I was giving my medical history, I told the examiner that I had a history of heart attack. He called Dr. Santucci, the Chairman of Internal Medicine and stopped the pre-employment exam until they did echocardiography and nuclear scan, where they found that I had heart disease and old heart attack. Dr. Santucci asked me to resign and look for a program in suburbs, where the work was more comfortable. I refused to quit when he said: if you refuse to quit we have to take you and will see what we can do. Residency training in the first year was monthly schedule; each resident had worked with an attending physician for the month of the schedule at the end of the month the physician wrote an evaluation for the resident.

They changed the schedule for the first month and put me with Dr. Murali. Dr. Murali is originally from India, specialist, internal medicine, and subspecialist in Immunology, and he had been working in Jamaica Hospital for about ten years. He was known as a friend of the Chairman. Two weeks later, the Chairman called me to his office in private. He said: We want you to resign and leave the program right now otherwise three of our attending physicians will write evaluations state that you are not valid to work as a physician so that we can remove you, but you will not practice medicine ever. I told him I was doing well and the attending physicians would write good evaluations. Dr. Santucci said: We have decided and the attending physicians will write bad evaluations anyway this is in our hand and very easy for us. I told him I could not leave. He said: you want to stay on our nose; we know how to kick you out.

I went hopeless, helpless in darkness. I had a non-working wife, three children, and heart disease. I could not return to Egypt because I was political asylee. All that I could do was just praying almighty God for a miracle. At that night, I had a dream that I was playing in a soccer game, while I had never played soccer in my real life. While I was acting as the goalkeeper, I shot the ball that passed the team to score a goal. The judge did not consider it a goal because I had shot before he gave start signal. After the official start, I decided to do the same act. I shot the ball, and I scored a goal, stated that it was the best goal in the history of soccer games. I understood that this was a signal that Almighty God might do a miracle.

The first month I worked with Dr. Murali. I had known that he would fabricate bad evaluation, so I was documenting everything. His evaluation is a discretional act; he did not need to present proof while I had to offer documented evidence that his evaluation was intentionally fabricated. When they introduced his evaluation to me for signing it as real, I signed as it was not right and presented a copy of charts of five patients, where I did better than him. One of these five cases, a patient was admitted for fall in the kitchen and had weakness in the right upper limb. Dr. Murali suggested it was a stroke, but I suggested he fall for syncope and the weakness was due to fracture neck. Dr. Murali did not wait for the result of CT scan and X-ray and discharged the patient to rehab for physical therapy as it was a case of stroke. The patient's condition got worse, and X-ray of his neck showed fracture neck. The patient was readmitted for stabilizing the neck and transferred out for emergency neurological surgery. The Chairman stayed three days in his office without showing up and gave notice to Dr. Murali to find another job. He found a job in Boston, MA and left his family and home in New York, for Boston job.

The second month was with Dr. Mark Adler, who was an elite young man, about ten years younger than me. He was known as related to the Chairman somehow, or he might be the boyfriend of the Chairman's daughter. Dr. Adler was supposed to write the second bad evaluation, and he did.

As usual, the admitted patient; first was seen by the attending physician and then by the senior resident then by the junior resident. Since I was the junior resident, I was the last one to see the patient. About 60 years old lady was admitted to the regular floor for Pneumonia. The senior resident took footsteps of Dr. Adler and diagnosed her with Pneumonia. Even her primary care physician visited her in the Hospital and took the footsteps of Dr. Adler and diagnosed her Pneumonia. When I saw the patient, I noticed that she had infected burn wound in her arm caused septicemia, fever and high white blood cells that possible mislead Dr. Adler so that he diagnosed her Pneumonia. Chest X-ray of severe Pneumonia is similar to that of the heart attack with congestive heart failure. I ordered a test for diagnosing the heart attack. At three am the test result came positive for severe heart attack. Before we transferred the patient to the Intensive Care, I called my wife to tell her I achieved the second soccer game goal. Dr. Adler had resigned for work in private practice.

The attending physicians had known that it was risky to satisfy the Chairman needs and fabricate any further false evaluations. One attending physician stated that his license was more important than the job. At the end of the education year, during the yearly Department Counsel Meeting, Dr. Santucci asked the Counsel to remove me from the program. Since most of the members had known that this case would go to the court they refused to sign and stated that in the monthly exams, even I was the first-year resident, I had been doing not only better than all of the first and second year residents but most of the third year residents as well. The Chairman suggested doing an election. Four out of 28 members voted for my removal. The Chairman stated that since some members did not want me in the program; I should be removed.

The director of the hospital and co-owner interfered against the Chairman to save the Hospital from discrimination case would deprive the Hospital of Medicare support and suggested that due to the conflict with the Chairman, they would find a position to me in another hospital or they keep me in the program. Even they saw a post in a program in another hospital they decided to keep me in their program as they feared I might get the position and still file a complaint about discrimination. After I had secured my place for the second year, I did angioplasty for my heart at St. Francis Hospital. My health became better.

I stayed open eyes, suffering from harassments to the end of the three-year training. The attending physician, who could bring a real case against me, would be a hero.

The third-year resident, at night, takes the duty of the attending physician. In one night in the first week of the third year, at 2 am, the emergency room had given me unstable patient for admission. The patient was collapsing. We intubated her and put her under mechanical respiration, but she was still collapsing. She had severe acidosis making acute heart failure, but acidosis due to chronic renal failure could be corrected only by dialysis, which was not available within minutes or intravenous Bicarbonate drip. The patient had a history of Chronic Kidney Disease, but she was not on dialysis yet. I started Bicarbonate drip. The patient acidosis was corrected, and the patient improved, and her life was saved. The patient was admitted to the intensive care. Dr. Patel, the Chief of Intensive Care and Dr. Mohammed Babury, next morning, complained to the Chairman that I gave the patient wrong medicine. The Chairman felt happy and called me to the physicians' lounge before all of the Attending Physicians told me I had to write for why I gave Bicarbonate drip, and if he found me did wrong, he would have no excuse to keep me in the program. Next day I had brought a copy from the patient chart showing the patient's condition got worse after they stopped the Bicarbonate drip and copy of pages from Nephrology textbook showing that I did not do only the right thing, but there was no other mean to save the life of the patient. Intensive care doctors were confused because the problem was more Nephrology than Intensive Care. The Chairman consulted a professor of nephrology from outside of the hospital, who gave a lecture to all of the Attending Physicians and the Residents about management of metabolic acidosis in emergency situations.

They deprived me of training in Mortality and Morbidity course. This training was for review the charts of the dead patients to see if it was possible to salvage their lives. They did that so that I did not know the hospital privacy of malpractice.

CHAPTER 3

New York Federal Court Order

◆ ◆ ◆

After graduation, I moved along with my family to Michigan, and I filed a complaint in the Federal District Court for all acts of discrimination including what is mentioned here. First, the Court granted them summary disposition in part. It dismissed all of the claims for they were time-barred as they were filed after more than 300 days except for one claim that they deprived me of training in Mortality and Morbidity training as it was not time-barred. The remaining claim, even it was not time-barred, it was dismissed later for I did not bring substantial evidence proved damage from I was deprived of taking Mortality and Morbidity training course.

The Court approved publishing its order online. The Court order is available online under title: E.D.N.Y. no. 04-3389. Hon. Judge Gleeson. {Youssef v. Jamaica Hospital Medical Center}.

Slip Copy, 2006 WL 3197184 (E.D.N.Y.)
Only the Westlaw citation is currently available.
FOR ONLINE PUBLICATION ONLY

United States District Court,
E.D. New York.

Abdelbaset A. YOUSSEF, Plaintiff,

v.

JAMAICA HOSPITAL MEDICAL CENTER, Defendant.

No. 04 CV 3389. Nov. 5, 2006.

Abdelbaset A. Youssef, Inkster, MI, Plaintiff, pro se.

Wilson, Elser, Moskowitz, Edelman & Dicker LLP, by Celena R Mayo, New York, NY, for Defendant.

MEMORANDUM AND ORDER

JOHN GLEESON, United States District Judge.

This is my second memorandum and order in Abdelbaset A. Youssef's action under the Americans with Disabilities Act of 1990, 42 U.S.C. §§ 12101 et seq. (2000), ("the ADA") against Jamaica Hospital Medical Center ("the Hospital"). Youssef claims the Hospital discriminated against him on account of a perceived disability while he was a resident there. I assume familiarity with my previous decision, filed April 18, 2005, which narrowed the case to a single issue: whether the Hospital discriminatorily denied Youssef Mortality and Morbidity ("M & M") training during his third year as a resident. Youssef has moved for summary judgment on this issue, [FN1] and the Hospital has brought a cross-motion. I conclude that even on Youssef's version of the facts, he cannot establish a prima facie case of discrimination under the ADA. Accordingly, I grant the Hospital's motion for summary judgment and deny Youssef's motion. [FN2]

FN1. Many of the arguments in Youssef's motion papers go to claims that I have already dismissed or issues not relevant to whether the Hospital is liable for depriving Youssef of M & M training. To the extent possible I will honor Youssef's request that I construe these arguments as bearing on the issue before me. See Memo of Law in Supp. Of Pl. Rule 56 Motion for Summary. J. ("Pl.'s Br.") at 1. However, some of the arguments are irredeemably about damages, see id. 11-13, 20, other remedies, see id. 16, 21, are time-barred claims, none of which are before me. On the latter topic, Youssef attempts to resurrect his claims regarding the Hospital's "false evaluations" on the grounds that the Hospital sent those evaluations to him for his signature on September 24, 2000. See, e.g., id. 17; see also 18 (claiming that an evaluation stating Youssef was "not valid to stay in the program" sprang from the discriminatory animus of "28 Attendings" and "the Chairman of the program"). As I explained in my previous memorandum and order, Youssef may not import time-barred allegations of discriminatory acts into the 300 day period by relating them to acts within that period. See Nat'l R.R. Passenger Corp. v. Morgan, 536 U.S. 101, 113 (2002). Accordingly, I do not address Youssef's claims about the "false evaluations." FN2. I, therefore, do not discuss the other arguments advanced by the Hospital in support of its motion.

Background

I assume familiarity with Youssef's version of the basic facts of his action, which I outlined in my previous memorandum and order. That outline will serve as background for the following facts taken from the record before me, construed with all inferences and disputes resolved in favor of the plaintiff.

On September 2, 2002, Youssef went to the office of the program director to ask for sick leave to undergo a medical procedure for his heart condition. While Youssef was there, he discovered that the posted schedule for M & M training had every resident in his program assigned to a four week round except him. M & M training is a four-week training course in which residents are paired with attending physicians to investigate patient deaths in the past four-week period. The pairs then present the results of one or two cases at a one hour conference. As a result of the Hospital's omission, Youssef was able to attend the conferences, but could not participate in the training or the conference presentations.

Youssef alleges that the Hospital omitted him from the schedule in "retaliation for my refusal to resign...." Pl.'s Opp'n and Reply 10. In July 2000, the Chairman of the Department of Medicine had advised Youssef, in light of his heart condition, to look for a less stressful job. When Youssef had declined, the Chairman had stated the Hospital would "have to take you for this year, and we will see."

Youssef did not object to the omission from the M & M training schedule, or request to be included in the training because his priority was simply to graduate successfully without provoking further discriminatory action against him. Nevertheless, he alleges that the consequences of the omission are severe. Without M & M training "no physician can work as [an] attending physician in a Hospital, or seek higher training." Id. 11.

Despite the deprivation, Youssef graduated from the program and now had medical privileges at two Oakwood Healthcare Systems affiliated hospitals. He also received certification from the American Board of Internal Medicine. He works in private practice making a yearly salary of $80,000, which he alleges is half the average hospital job salary and less than a third of a specialist's salary. Despite applying to internist positions at ten physician employment agencies, Youssef received no offers. Youssef claims his inability to acquire the jobs yielding those higher salaries is due to his lack of M & M training.

The Hospital suggests it has never received inquiries specifically about the lack of Youssef's M & M training and Youssef can point to no such inquiries. Nevertheless, Youssef claims the Hospital has received many requests for this information from prospective hospital employers: "Whenever I apply for a job or training the company would send a confidential request about my training history, and it will be illegal for Jamaica Hospital to hide this shameful record." Pl.'s Br. 19. Youssef suggests that the Hospital illegally hides the M & M training information from prospective employers (and, presumably, the Court) out of fear that the employer would litigate the matter. See id. In the alternative, Youssef claims the Hospital hands over the information but then destroys the correspondence at the request of the prospective employers. See Pl.'s Opp'n and Reply 14A. Youssef also claims the Hospital may have simply lost the information. See id. 14C.

Discussion

A moving party may obtain summary judgment if the record demonstrates no genuine issue of material fact such that the party is entitled to judgment as a matter of law. Fed. R. Civ. P. 56(c). "[T]he inferences to be drawn from the underlying facts ... must be viewed in the light most favorable to the party opposing the motion." Matsushita Elec. Indus. Co. v. Zenith Radio Corp., 475 U.S. 574, 587 (1986) (quotation marks and citation omitted). Casting merely "metaphysical doubt" upon the evidence produced by the moving party will not defeat a motion for summary judgment; however, the factual dispute must be genuine. Matsushita, 475 U .S. at 586.

The Second Circuit applies the burden-shifting scheme of McDonnell Douglas Corp. v. Green, 411 U.S. 792 (1973), to disability discrimination claims pursuant to the ADA. Heyman v. Queens Vill. Comm. for Mental Health, 198 F.3d 68, 72 (2d Cir.1999). "McDonnell Douglas and subsequent decisions have 'established an allocation of the burden of production and an order for the presentation of proof in ... discriminatory treatment cases.' Reeves v. Sanderson Plumbing Prods., Inc., 530 U.S. 133, 142 (2000) (quoting St. Mary's Honor Ctr. v. Hicks, 509 U.S. 502, 506 (1993)). A prima facie case for a discrimination claim under the ADA requires, inter alia, the plaintiff to produce evidence that he suffered an adverse employment action because of his disability. See Heyman, 198 F.3d at 72. For claims of employment discrimination against members of a protected class, an adverse employment action is one that causes the aggrieved employee to suffer a materially adverse change in employment status or the terms and conditions of employment. See Kessler v. Westchester County Dep't of Soc. Serves., 461 F.3d 199, 207 (2d Cir.2006) (discussing the "adverse employment action" standard for discrimination claims pursuant to Title VII of the Civil Rights Act of 1964, 42 U.S.C. §§ 2000e et seq. (2000), and the Age Discrimination in Employment Act of 1967, 29 U.S.C. §§ 621 et seq. (2000)).

The Hospital argues that Youssef has not made out a prima facie case on his discrimination claim, in part because he lacks evidence that the alleged discrimination on the part of the Hospital resulted in an adverse employment action against him. Specifically, it claims that Youssef has failed to adduce evidence from which a jury could infer that the Hospital's alleged failure to include him in M & M training caused a materially adverse change in the terms and conditions of Youssef's employment.

Youssef's adverse employment action argument reduces to two claims: (1) the deprivation of M & M training caused him to take a lower salary than he would have otherwise, and (2) the deprivation of training caused him to lose opportunities for employment in hospitals and more advanced training. A decreased post-residency salary and lost job opportunities are likely materially adverse harms to a medical resident. [FN3] Accordingly, the harm Youssef alleges would likely make the Hospital's deprivation of M & M training an adverse employment action, had Youssef satisfied his burden of producing evidence about the cause of the harm. But Youssef produces no admissible evidence that the deprivation of M & M training caused the harms he complains of.

FN3. Medical residents are both employees and students training for employment as doctors. See Def.'s Local R. 56.1 Statement 2 (noting that the Hospital's "Residency Training Program is a hybrid post-graduate educational/employment program for medical students"). Accordingly, the material damage wrought upon Youssef's employability such as the loss in potential salary and job opportunities alleged here was also material damage to his employment status as a resident.

On the first claim, I assume Youssef is correct that physicians in private practice receive only half the salary a hospital job would pay and a third the salary of a specialist. I will also assume Youssef is correct that without M & M training no doctor can work as an attending physician in a hospital or receive higher training. But Youssef requires something besides his own bare statements that with the Hospital's M & M training he would have been accepted as an attending physician. Youssef has advanced no admissible evidence supporting that inference.

Youssef also claims his lack of M & M training has denied him opportunities as an internist or trainee.

But again, he provides no evidence for the causal link that supports his claim. Indeed, Youssef himself entertains the theory that his potential employers were not even on notice about his lack of M & M training, i.e., he claims it is possible that the Hospital either concealed or lost the information. But even assuming Youssef's alternative theory is true that the Hospital provides the information but then conceals the correspondence the record is utterly devoid of evidence that his lack of training is responsible for the employers' lack of interest. Indeed, Youssef's repeated reminders that he endured negative evaluations during his tenure at the Hospital help demonstrate that even if the lack of M & M training was disclosed to his prospective employers, it is scarcely plausible that it had anything to do with disqualifying Youssef from those jobs.

To be sure, the counterfactual evidence is often, perhaps mostly, circumstantial. But Youssef had plenty of opportunity during discovery to obtain some evidence on this issue to put before the Court: statistics on the qualifications of internists, for example, or expert testimony on the relative importance of M & M training for newly graduated residents, or even a sampling of his rejection letters. His suppositions about what motivated potential employers, no matter how frequently Youssef repeats them, are no substitute for admissible evidence supporting his claim that M & M training would have resulted in him obtaining a higher salary or additional employment opportunities. Accordingly, Youssef's ADA claim fails because he has produced insufficient evidence to support his allegation of discrimination.

Conclusion

For the reasons articulated above, the defendant's cross-motion for summary judgment is granted, and the plaintiff's motion is denied.

So ordered.

1:04-cv-03389 (Docket) (Aug. 9, 2004)

END OF DOCUMENT

CHAPTER 4

Chronic Pain Syndrome

◆ ◆ ◆

CHRONIC PAIN IS PAIN THAT lasts a long time. In medicine, the distinction between acute and chronic pain is sometimes determined by an arbitrary interval of time since onset; the two most commonly used markers being three months and six months since onset, though some theorists and researchers have placed the transition from acute to chronic pain at 12 months. Others apply acute to pain that lasts less than 30 days, chronic to pain of more than six months duration, and subacute to pain that lasts from one to six months. A popular alternative definition of chronic pain, involving no arbitrarily fixed length, is "pain that extends beyond the expected period of healing." Epidemiological studies have found that 10.1% to 55.2% of people in various countries have chronic pain.

Chronic pain may originate in the body, or in the brain or spinal cord. It is often difficult to treat. Various non-opioid medicines are recommended initially, depending on whether the pain originates from tissue damage or is neuropathic. Psychological treatments including cognitive behavioral therapy and acceptance and commitment therapy may be effective for improving quality of life in those with chronic pain. Some people with chronic pain may benefit from opioid treatment while others are harmed. A trial of opioids is only recommended in those with non-cancer pain; who has no history of either mental illness or substance use disorder and should be stopped if not effective.

Severe chronic pain is associated with increased 10-year mortality, particularly from heart disease and respiratory disease. People with chronic pain tend to have higher rates of depression, anxiety, and sleep disturbances; these are correlations, and it is often not clear which factor causes another. Chronic pain may contribute to decreased physical activity due to fear of exacerbating pain, often resulting in weight gain. Pain intensity, pain control, and resiliency to pain are influenced by different levels and types of social support that a person with chronic pain receives.

The International Association for the study of pain defines chronic pain as pain with no biological value that persists past normal tissue healing. The DSM-5 recognizes one chronic pain disorder, somatic symptom disorders, and reduction of the three previously recognized pain disorders. The criteria include it lasting for greater than six months.

The suggested ICD-11 chronic pain classification suggests seven categories of chronic pain.

1. Chronic primary pain: defined by three months of persistent pain in one or more anatomical regions that are unexplainable by another pain condition.
2. Chronic cancer pain: defined as cancer or treatment-related visceral, musculoskeletal, or bony pain.
3. Chronic posttraumatic pain: pain lasting three months post trauma or surgery, excluding infectious or preexisting conditions.

4. Chronic neuropathic pain: pain caused by damage to the somato-sensory nervous system damage.
5. A chronic headache and oro-facial pain: pain that originates in the head or face, and occurs for 50% or more days over a three months period.
6. Chronic visceral pain: pain originating in an internal organ.
7. Chronic musculoskeletal pain: pain originating in the bones, muscles, joints or connective tissue.

Chronic pain may be divided into "nociceptive" (caused by inflamed or damaged tissue activating specialized pain sensors called nociceptors and "neuropathic" (caused by damage to or malfunction of the nervous system).

Nociceptive pain may be divided into "superficial" and "deep," and deep pain into deep somatic and visceral. Superficial pain is initiated by activation of nociceptors in the skin or superficial tissues. Deep somatic pain is initiated by stimulation of nociceptors in ligaments, tendons, bones, blood vessels, fasciae, and muscles, and is dull, aching, poorly localized pain. Visceral pain originates in the viscera (organs). Visceral pain may be well localized, but often it is extremely difficult to locate, and several visceral regions produce "referred" pain when damaged or inflamed, where the sensation is located in an area distant from the site of pathology or injury.

Neuropathic pain is divided into "peripheral" (originating in the peripheral nervous system) and "central" (originating in the brain or spinal cord). Peripheral neuropathic pain is often described as "burning," "tingling," "electrical," "stabbing," or "pins and needles."

Under persistent activation, nociceptive transmission to the dorsal horn may induce a pain phenomenon. This induces pathological changes that lower the threshold for pain signals to be transmitted. Also, it may generate non-nociceptive nerve fibers to respond to pain signals. Non-nociceptive nerve fibers may also be able to generate and transmit pain signals. The type of nerve fibers that are believed to propagate the pain signals are the C-fibers since they have a slow conductivity and give rise to a painful sensation that persists for a long time. In chronic pain, this process is difficult to reverse or eradicate once established. In some cases, chronic pain can be caused by genetic factors which interfere with neuronal differentiation, leading to a permanent reduction in the threshold for pain.

Chronic pain of different etiologies has been characterized as a disease affecting brain structure, and MRI studies have shown abnormal anatomical and functional connectivity, even during rest involving areas related to the processing of pain. Also, persistent pain has been shown to cause gray matter loss, reversible once the pain has resolved.

These structural changes can be explained by the phenomenon known as neuroplasticity. In the case of chronic pain, the somatotopic representation of the body is inappropriately reorganized following peripheral and central sensitization. This maladaptive change results in the experience of allodynia or_hyperalgesia. Brain activity in individuals with chronic pain, measured by (EEG), has been demonstrated to be altered, suggesting pain-induced neuroplastic changes. More specifically, the relative beta activity (compared to the rest of the brain) is increased, the relative alpha activity is decreased, and the theta activity both absolutely and relatively is diminished.

Dopaminergic dysfunction has been hypothesized to act as a shared mechanism between chronic pain, insomnia, and major depressive disorder. Increased tonic dopamine activity and a compensatory decrease in phasic dopamine activity, which is important in inhibiting pain. This is supported by the implication of catecholamine in fibromyalgia and temporomandibular joint syndrome. Astrocytes Microglia and Satellite glial cells have been found to be dysfunctional in chronic pain. Increased activity of microglia and alterations of microglial networks as well as increased production of chemokines and cytokines by microglia are proposed to act to potentiate pain. Astrocytes have been observed to lose their ability to regulate the excitability of neurons, increasing spontaneous neural activity in pain circuits.

Pain Management

Pain management is the branch of medicine employing an interdisciplinary approach to the relief of pain and improvement in the quality of life of those living with pain. The typical pain management team includes medical practitioners (particularly anesthesiologists, clinical psychologists, physician assistants, and nurse practitioners. Acute pain usually resolves with the efforts of one practitioner; however, the management of chronic pain frequently requires the coordinated efforts of the treatment team. Complete and sustained remission of many types of chronic pain is rare, though some can be done to improve quality of life.

Non-Opioids

Initially recommended efforts are non-opioid based therapies. Various non-opioid medicines are used, depending on whether the pain originates from tissue damage or is neuropathic. Limited evidence suggests that chronic pain from tissue inflammation or damage (as in rheumatoid arthritis and cancer pain) is best treated with opioids, while for neuropathic pain (pain caused by a damaged or dysfunctional nervous system) other drugs may be more effective, such as antidepressants and anticonvulsants.

Because of weak evidence, the best approach is not clear when treating many types of pain, and doctors must rely on their own clinical experience. Doctors often cannot predict who will use opioids just for pain management and who will go on to develop an addiction, and cannot always distinguish between those who are and those who are not seeking opioids due primarily to an existing addiction. Withholding, interrupting or withdrawing opioid treatment in people who benefit from it can cause harm.

While there is no high-quality evidence to support ultrasound, it has been found to have a small effect on improving function in nonspecific chronic low back pain.

While exercise has been offered as a method to lessen chronic pain and there is some evidence of benefit, this evidence is tentative. Side effects of exercise are few in this population.

Opioids

In those who have not benefited from other measures and have no history of either mental illness or substance use disorder treatment with opioids may be tried. If the significant benefit does not occur, it is recommended that they are stopped. In those on opioids, stopping or decreasing their use may improve outcomes including pain.

Some people with chronic pain benefit from opioid treatment and others do not; the treatment harms some. Possible harms include reduced sex hormone production, hypogonadism, infertility, impaired immune system, falls and fractures in older adults, neonatal abstinence syndrome, heart problems, sleep-disordered breathing, opioid-induced hyperalgesia, physical dependence, addiction, and overdose.

Alternative Medicine

Hypnosis, including self-hypnosis, has tentative evidence. Evidence does not support hypnosis for chronic pain due to a spinal cord injury. Preliminary studies have found medical marijuana to be beneficial in treating neuropathic pain, but not other kinds of long-term pain. Further research is needed.

Tai Chi has been shown to improve pain, stiffness, and quality of life in chronic conditions such as osteoarthritis, low back pain, and osteoporosis. Acupuncture has also been found to be an effective and safe treatment for reducing pain and improving quality of life for chronic pelvic pain syndrome specifically.

High-quality evidence does not currently support Trans-cranial magnetic stimulation for reduction of chronic pain, and the demonstrated effects are small and short-term.

Epidemiology

A systematic literature review of chronic pain found that the prevalence of chronic pain varied in various countries from 10.1% to 55.2% of the population, affected women at a higher rate than men, and that chronic pain consumes a large number of healthcare resources around the globe.

A large-scale telephone survey of 15 European countries and Israel, 19% of respondents over 18 years of age, had suffered pain for more than six months, including the last month. More than twice in the previous week, with pain intensity of 5 or more for the last episode, on a scale of 1 (no pain) to 10 (worst imaginable). 4839 of these respondents with chronic pain were interviewed in depth. Sixty-six percent scored their pain intensity at moderate (5–7), and 34% at severe (8–10); 46% had constant pain, 56% intermittent; 49% had suffered pain for 2–15 years; and 21% had been diagnosed with depression due to the pain. Sixty-one percent were unable or less able to work outside the home, 19% had lost a job, and 13% had changed jobs due to their pain. Forty percent had inadequate pain management, and less than 2% were seeing a pain management specialist.

In the United States, the prevalence of chronic pain has been estimated to be approximately 35%, with approximately 50 million Americans experiencing partial or total disability as a consequence. According to the Institute of Medicine, about 116 million Americans are living with chronic pain, which suggests that approximately half of American adults have some chronic pain condition. The Mayday Fund estimate of 70 million Americans with chronic pain is slightly more conservative. In an internet study, the prevalence of chronic pain in the United States was calculated to be 30.7% of the population: 34.3% for women and 26.7% for men.

Outcome

Chronic pain is associated with higher rates of depression and anxiety. Those with chronic pain often experience sleep disturbance and insomnia due to medication and illness symptoms. Chronic pain may contribute to decreased physical activity due to fear of exacerbating pain, often resulting in weight gain. Such co-morbidities can be difficult to treat due to the high potential of medication interactions, especially when different doctors treat the conditions.

Severe chronic pain is associated with increased 10-year mortality, particularly from heart disease and respiratory disease. Several mechanisms have been proposed for the increased mortality, e.g., abnormal endocrine stress response. Additionally, chronic stress seems to affect cardiovascular risk by the acceleration of the atherosclerotic process. However, further research is needed to clarify the relationship between severe chronic pain, stress and cardiovascular health levels. Self-esteem is often low in people with chronic pain, also shows striking improvement once pain has resolved.

It has been suggested that catastrophizing may play a role in the experience of pain. Pain catastrophizing is the tendency to describe a pain experience in more exaggerated terms than the average person, to think a great deal more about the pain when it occurs, or to feel more helpless about the experience. People who score highly on measures of catastrophization are likely to rate a pain experience as more intense than those who score low on such measures. It is often reasoned that the tendency to catastrophize causes the person to experience the pain as more intense. One suggestion is that catastrophizing influences pain perception through altering attention and anticipation and heightening emotional responses to pain. However, at least some aspects of catastrophization may be the product of intense pain experience, rather than its cause. That is, the more intense the pain feels to the person, the more likely they are to have thoughts about it that fit the definition of catastrophization.

Social Support

Social support has important consequences for individuals with chronic pain. In particular, pain intensity, pain control, and resiliency to pain have been implicated as outcomes influenced by different levels and types of social support. Much of this research has focused on emotional, instrumental, tangible and informational social support. People with persistent pain conditions tend to rely on their social support as a coping mechanism and therefore have better outcomes when they are a part of larger more supportive social networks. Across a majority of studies investigated, there was a significant direct association between social activities or social support and pain. Higher levels of pain were associated with a decrease in social activities, lower levels of social support, and reduced social functioning.

Effect on Cognition

Chronic pain's impact on cognition is an under-researched area, but several tentative conclusions have been published. Most people with chronic pain complain of cognitive impairment, such as forgetfulness, difficulty with attention, and difficulty completing tasks. Objective testing has found that people in chronic pain tend to experience impairment in attention, memory, mental flexibility, verbal ability, the speed of response in a cognitive task, and speed in executing structured tasks.

Moderate to Severe Pain Management

Generally; pain management, pain medicine, or pain control is a branch of medicine employing an interdisciplinary approach for easing the suffering and improving the quality of life of those living with chronic or acute severe pain. Pain sometimes resolves promptly once the underlying trauma or pathology has healed, and is treated by one physician practitioner, with drugs such as analgesics and anxiolytics. Effective management of chronic, long-term pain, however, frequently requires the coordinated efforts of the management team.

Medicine treats injury and pathology to support and speed healing and treats distressing symptoms such as pain to relieve suffering during treatment and healing. When a painful injury or pathology is resistant to treatment and pain persists after the injury or pathology has healed, and medical science cannot identify the cause of pain, the task of medicine is to relieve suffering. Treatment often includes such as antidepressants, analgesics, anticonvulsants and interventional procedures, physical therapy, physical exercise, application of ice and heat, and psychological measures, such as biofeedback and cognitive behavioral therapy.

When treating moderate to severe pain, the type of the pain, acute or chronic, needs to be considered. The type of pain can result in different medications being prescribed. Certain medications may work better for acute pain, others for chronic pain, and some may work equally well on both. Acute pain medication is for rapid onset of pain such as from an inflicted trauma or to treat post-operative pain. Chronic pain medication is for alleviating long-lasting, ongoing pain.

Morphine is the gold standard to which all narcotics are compared Semi-synthetic derivatives of morphine such as hydromorphone (Dilaudid), oxymorphone (Opana), and others vary in such ways as the duration of action, side effect profile and milligram potency Fentanyl has the benefit of less histamine release and thus fewer side effects. It can also be administered via a transdermal patch which is convenient for chronic pain management. The FDA has approved various immediate-release fentanyl products for breakthrough cancer pain. Oxycodone is used across the Americas and Europe for the relief of serious chronic pain; its main slow release formula is known as OxyContin, and short-acting tablets, capsules, syrups, and ampules are available making it suitable for acute intractable pain or breakthrough pain, diamorphine methadone and buprenorphine are used less frequently. Pethidine, known in North America as meperidine, is not recommended for pain management due to its low potency, short duration of action, and toxicity associated with repeated use. Pentazocine and dextromoramide also not recommended in new patients except for acute pain where other analgesics are not tolerated or are inappropriate,

Drugs of other types can be used to help opioids combat certain types of pain, for example, amitriptyline is prescribed for chronic muscular pain in the arms, legs, neck and lower back with an opiate, or sometimes without it and with an NSAID.

While opiate is often used in the management of chronic pain, high doses are associated with an increased risk of opioid overdose.

Opioids

From the Food and Drug Administration's website: "According to the National Institute of Health, studies have shown that properly managed medical use of opioid analgesic compounds (taken exactly as prescribed) is safe, can manage pain effectively, and rarely causes addiction.

Opioid medications can provide short, intermediate or long-acting analgesia depending upon the specific properties of the medication and whether it is formulated as an extended release drug. Opioid medications may be administered orally, by injection, via nasal mucosa or oral mucosa, rectally, transdermally, intravenously, epidurally and intrathecally. In chronic pain conditions that are opioid responsive, a combination of a long-acting (OxyContin, MS Contin, Opana ER, Exalgo, and Methadone) or extended release medication is often prescribed in conjunction with a shorter-acting medication (oxycodone, morphine or hydromorphone) for breakthrough pain, or exacerbations.

The most opioid treatment used by patients outside of healthcare settings is oral (tablet, capsule or liquid) but suppositories and skin patches can be prescribed. An opioid injection is rarely needed for patients with chronic pain.

Although opioids are strong analgesics, they do not provide complete analgesia regardless of whether the pain is acute or chronic in origin. Opioids are efficacious analgesics in chronic malignant pain and modestly effective in nonmalignant pain management. However, there are associated adverse effects, especially during the commencement or change in dose. When opioids are used for prolonged period drug tolerance, chemical dependency, diversion, and addiction may occur.

Clinical guidelines for prescribing opioids for chronic pain have been issued by the American Pain Society and the American Academy of Pain Medicine. Included in these guidelines is the importance of assessing the patient for the risk of substance abuse, misuse, or addiction; a personal or family history of substance abuse is the strongest predictor of aberrant drug-taking behavior. Physicians who prescribe opioids should integrate this treatment with any psychotherapeutic intervention the patient may be receiving. The guidelines also recommend monitoring not only the pain but also the level of functioning and the achievement of therapeutic goals. The prescribing physician should be suspicious of abuse when a patient reports a reduction in pain but has no accompanying improvement in function or progress in achieving identified goals.

Non-Steroidal Anti-Inflammatory Drugs

The other major group of analgesics is non-steroidal anti-inflammatory drugs (NSAID). Acetaminophen is not always included in this class of medications. However, acetaminophen may be administered as a single medication or in combination with other analgesics (both NSAIDs and opioids). The alternatively prescribed NSAIDs such as Ketoprofen and Piroxicam have limited benefit in chronic pain disorders and with long-term use are associated with significant adverse effects. The use of selective NSAIDs designated as selective COX-2 inhibitors has significant cardiovascular and cerebrovascular risks which have limited their utilization.

Antidepressants And Antiepileptic Drugs

Some antidepressant and antiepileptic drugs are used in chronic pain management and act primarily within the pain pathways of the central nervous system, though peripheral mechanisms have been attributed as well. These mechanisms vary and in general are more effective in neuropathic pain disorders as well as complex regional pain syndrome. Drugs such as gabapentin have been widely prescribed for the off-label use of pain control. The list of side effects for these classes of drugs are typically much longer than opiate or NSAID treatments for chronic pain, and many anti-epileptics cannot be suddenly stopped without the risk of seizure.

Cannabinoids

Chronic pain is one of the most commonly cited reasons for the use of medical marijuana. A 2012 Canadian survey of participants in their medical marijuana program found that 84% of respondents reported using medical marijuana for the management of pain.

Evidence of medical marijuana's pain mitigating effects is conclusive. Detailed in a 1999 report by the Institute of Medicine, "the available evidence from animal and human studies indicates that cannabinoids can have a substantial analgesic effect." In a 2013 review study published in Fundamental & Clinical Pharmacology, various studies were cited in demonstrating that cannabinoids exhibit comparable effectiveness to opioids in models of acute pain and even greater effectiveness in models of chronic pain.

CHAPTER 5

Pain Management Challenges

◆ ◆ ◆

BEFORE I TALK ABOUT PAIN management challenges, I am presenting evidence that the Michigan State Legislature and Michigan Board of Medicine are aware of some of these challenges.

MICHIGAN COMPILED LAW;

MCL 333.16204(c) (1) The legislature finds that the use of controlled substances is appropriate in the medical treatment of specific forms of pain and that efforts to control diversion or improper administration of controlled substances should not interfere with the legitimate, medically recognized use of those controlled substances to relieve pain and suffering.

(2) The legislature finds that some patients in this state with pain are unable to obtain from their health care providers sufficient pain relief through the prescription of controlled substances, especially controlled substances included in schedule 2 under section 7214.

(3) It is the intent of the legislature to permit and facilitate adequate treatment for pain by licensed health professionals, including, but not limited to, the prescription or dispensing of controlled substances included in schedule 2 under section 7214, when medically appropriate, and to enable regulatory and law

enforcement agencies to prevent the abuse and diversion of controlled substances by creating an electronic monitoring system.

Board of Medicine: Guidelines for the Use of Controlled Substances for the Treatment of Pain Section I:

The Michigan Boards of Medicine and Osteopathic Medicine & Surgery recognize that principles of quality medical practice dictate that the people of the State of Michigan have access to appropriate and effective pain relief. The appropriate application of up-to-date knowledge and treatment modalities can serve to improve the quality of life for those patients who suffer from pain as well as reduce the morbidity and costs associated with untreated or inappropriately treated pain.

The Board encourages physicians to view effective pain management as a part of quality medical practice for all patients with pain, acute or chronic, and it is especially important for patients who experience pain as a result of terminal illness.

All physicians should become knowledgeable about effective methods of pain treatment as well as statutory requirements for prescribing controlled substances. Inadequate pain control may result from physicians' lack of knowledge about pain management or an inadequate understanding of addiction. Fears of investigation or sanction by federal, state and local regulatory agencies may also result in inappropriate or inadequate treatment of chronic pain patients. Accordingly, these guidelines have been developed to clarify the Boards' position on pain control, specifically as related to the use of controlled substances, to alleviate physician uncertainty and to encourage better pain management. The Boards recognize that controlled substances, including opioid analgesics, may be essential in the treatment of acute pain due to trauma or surgery and chronic pain, whether due to cancer or non-cancer origins.

Physicians are referred to the U.S. Agency for Health Care and Research Clinical Practice Guidelines for a sound approach to the management of acute and cancer-related pain. The medical management of pain should be based on current knowledge and research and include the use of both pharmacologic and non-pharmacologic modalities. Pain should be assessed and treated promptly, and the quantity and frequency of doses should be adjusted according to the intensity and duration of the pain. Physicians should recognize that tolerance and physical dependence are normal consequences of sustained use of opioid analgesics and are not synonymous with addiction.

The Boards are obligated under the laws of the State of Michigan to protect the public health and safety. The Boards recognize that inappropriate prescribing of controlled substances, including opioid analgesics, may lead to drug diversion and abuse by individuals who seek them for other than legitimate medical use. Physicians should be diligent in preventing the diversion of drugs for illegitimate purposes.

Physicians should not fear disciplinary action from the Board or the other state regulatory or enforcement agency for prescribing, dispensing or administering controlled substances, including opioid analgesics, for a legitimate medical purpose and in the usual course of professional practice. The Board will consider prescribing, ordering, administering or dispensing controlled substances for pain to be for a legitimate medical purpose if based on accepted scientific knowledge of the treatment of pain or if based on sound clinical grounds.

All such prescribing must be based on clear documentation of unrelieved pain and in compliance with applicable state or federal law. Each case of prescribing for pain will be evaluated on an individual basis. The board will not take disciplinary action against a physician for failing to adhere strictly to the provisions of these guidelines if good cause is shown for such deviation. The physician's conduct will be evaluated to a great extent by the treatment outcome, taking into account whether the drug used is medically and/or pharmacologically recognized to be appropriate for the diagnosis, the patient's individual needs including any improvement in functioning and recognizing that some types of pain cannot be completely relieved.

The Boards will judge the validity of prescribing based on the physician's treatment of the patient and available documentation, rather than on the quantity and chronicity of prescribing. The goal is to control the patient's pain for its duration while effectively addressing other aspects of the patient's functioning, including physical, psychological, social and work-related factors. The following guidelines are not intended to define complete or best practice, but rather to communicate what the Boards consider to be within the boundaries of professional practice.

From my Experience

I had been practicing Dermatology and Internal Medicine for more than 30 years. Currently, I am a specialist in Internal Medicine. For the last ten years, I dedicated my work to patients who have severe disabling chronic pain syndrome. Since I am an internist, I had been treating all of the other medical problems along with pain. I had been selecting my patients with stringent criteria. The patient should be older than 30 years; however, most of them are older than 50 years, have a record of entirely documented disabling severe lifelong chronic pain syndrome, and he likely needs narcotic medicine all of his life. Most of my patients are officially disable and have Medicare insurance for their physical disability. Many patients had been my patients, who were stable functioning well and working for more than ten years. Some of my patients were for addiction treatment.

In Michigan, there is a very severe shortage of physicians prescribing pain medicine, not only due to fear from investigation or sanction as stated in the Board's guidelines and legislature but also due to the patients' factors. Pain is unlike all of the other diseases such as fever and renal disease, could be documented by specific lab results. Pain is subjective; every patient has his justification for particular pain medication needs, and he thinks his pain is the worst. Even though he can do, but it is not easy for a physician to give narcotics to selected patients among his other patients, who have pain as well. He would be accused of discriminating some of his patients.

When a physician dedicates his work to treat only patients with chronic pain syndrome, he has the privilege to put criteria for giving pain medicine without he would be accused of discrimination. In the other side, acute pain is better treated in the urgent care, walk-in clinic or emergency room so that the patient will not claim the physician is responsible for giving him narcotics for the length of the period he wants rather than the period he needs as his primary care physician. I suggest that primary care office is assigned to be for either regular patients; no pain medicine or it is restricted to patients with severe chronic lifelong pain syndrome. In this way, the pain doctor will be able to put his criteria for giving controlled medicine without intimidation or accusing of discrimination.

Sound pain management practically is available to wealthy or Medicare people only. Rich people have good insurance and money. Pain centers take good insurance or cash patients, who can pay high visit fee and pay for costly medicine and costly procedures. Some pain clinics; sometimes do procedures such risky spinal epidural injections just to justify giving narcotics to satisfy the Board of Medicine requirement for non-pharmacologic treatment or other reasons. Some patients may accept having spinal injections so that they could take narcotic prescriptions. Physicians more likely give narcotics to high socioeconomic people because they are unlikely abusing the system such as asking for medication, which is not needed, sell their medications, or mislead the doctors. Poor patients may sell part or all of their medications even they need it for buying food for example. The rich or high socioeconomic people often fear from the law enforcement agencies; as they are highly educated and have sensitive jobs. Accordingly, the rich and the upper socioeconomic people are easily securing their pain management needs; even they may be over treated.

Wealthy people often will become poor once they get disabling chronic pain syndrome. Poor patients, who do not have Medicare, either have Medicaid Insurance but no money or nothing at all. Poor patients, who do not have Medicaid practically, do not have access to sound pain management. For example; the poor patient could pay $50 for a primary care visit and get six month supply of cheap blood pressure medicine. For pain management, he needs $200 for a monthly visit to the pain center, cost of drug screening and others. The pain doctor shall refer him to expensive physical therapy, $2000 worse MRI and many other procedures, even they did not need it, so that he may document justification of giving narcotics or otherwise.

Patients, who get Medicaid, have it through Health Maintenance Organizations {HMO} plans. Through HMO, he can only see his primary care physician. The HMO primary care physician often does not give pain medicine or transfer to a pain clinic, which usually does not take HMO insurances as well.

One night I was called to psychiatry inpatient floor in Heritage Hospital, to see patient has a nervous breakdown. The patient was 60 years old, was released from the prison for Cocaine case. In prison, he had back surgery and had been given narcotic pain medicine. After he was released, he was given Medicaid (HMO) insurance. His HMO primary care physician refused to provide him with pain medicine. He kept changing the primary care physicians and changing the plans. In the office of the last primary care physician, he saw signs on the four sides of the waiting room stating no narcotics. He ended in nervous breakdown inside the office; the ambulance took him to be admitted to the psych floor. He had been keeping crying on the psych floor as a patient with psychosis. He had no money or good insurance, and he had a history of imprisonment for a drug-related case so that he was not able to secure pain management. His dream was going back to the prison. It is not recommended to give narcotics to a patient with a history of substance abuse, so there are significant ethical questions about those patients' rights of pain management. The recommendation is that we do not give narcotic to this kind of patients, how about their constitutional rights of treatment.

Due to she did not have proper insurance, on 10/29/2013, patient N. M., she was 32 years old lady, has Medicaid / HMO insurance, came to my office after she visited five emergency rooms in 5 hospitals. One of these hospitals was the University of Michigan, which one of the best hospitals nationwide. She had pain and weakness in the left lower limb. Each emergency room of the five-hospital recommended physical therapy. After she had given up treatment in the emergency rooms, she came to my office hopeless helpless as she had known that her case was an emergency room matter, while my office was not urgent care. I suggested a provisional diagnosis of either spinal abscess or acute herniated spinal disc. I referred her to Oakwood Hospital Medical Center with strongly supportive referral and planned for management. She reached the hospital with a critical condition, and they found she had MRSA abscess in the Hip joint and due to delayed management, she ended with a septic shock. She stayed for six-month treatment in the Hospital and a nursing home for intravenous Vancomycin. After she was released, it took about one year to find one orthopedic surgeon took her insurance, but he refused to do a total hip replacement for the surgery, due to scaring, was risky. I referred her to University of Michigan (U of M), as they have to take her insurance. U of M had been sending her for six months waiting after another six months waiting until my office had been closed. Next is my referral to Oakwood Hospital.

Astoria Medical
Abdelbaset A Youssef, MD

To: ER of any Hospital 10/29/2013
Re: N**** M*****
She has a sudden onset of back pain and complete paralysis of the left lower limb. Physical therapy will not help, even it may make it worse.

She needs Emergency admission and Emergency MRI; she may need Emergency Back Surgery to save her lower limb and her life.

I will not give her treatment or pain medicine today until I got a clear answer from the ER.

Abdelbaset A Youssef
Cell phone 24 hours, (313) 645 ****.

◆ ◆ ◆

Patients often share their medicine with spouses who need pain medicine as well. In the past, Medicare insurance had not covered medications, some patients pay for pain medicine, but they did not pay for blood pressure medicine. I saw patient, he almost lose his kidney due to neglected hypertension but his Kidney improved after Medicare have started to cover medication.

Patients, who were not able to secure their addiction treatment for they did not have insurance, buy Suboxone cheaper from other patients to self-treat themselves. One patient, on addiction treatment, told me that prescription narcotics come from Mexico in huge jars. Addiction physicians, treating addiction, follow the directions of the state pharmacist, who often carries old pharmacy degree that currently is not offered by any college. They are, for a long time, away from practicing medicine or pharmacy against the standard medical practice and medical ethics to avoid sanction. This act prejudices the patients. For example, patient addicted to heroin went to addiction clinics; they found Xanax in her urine. Once she was rejected from one clinic could not be accepted in any other clinic. She was deprived of treatment. Where she go? The young lady was very eager for treatment. She took Xanax because it was available to replace heroin, which was not available. She did very well on Suboxone, she was very happy and started functioning and was doing very well in her work until my office was closed. I do not know how she is doing now.

Young people, who have chronic pain syndrome, are undertreated because the young people are more likely abuse the system and many of them are troublemakers. All doctors including myself have been avoiding dealing with the young patient in pain management. The young patients pay the price for their age mates' wrongful acts.

Among many other challenges, that is very often; pharmacies refuse to fill narcotic prescriptions for Medicaid patients, because Medicaid pays a very low margin of profit, while the pharmacies are trying to avoid dispensing narcotics as they could. Pharmacies claim that narcotic prescription is legal and security load on the pharmacies, so they have to fill it along with non-narcotic prescriptions or for reasonable profit as in cash sale to balance the risk of carrying narcotic in the pharmacy. The criminals attack the pharmacy often for narcotics.

CHAPTER 6

Hypocrisy of the Board of Medicine

◆ ◆ ◆

THE BOARD OF MEDICINE IS authorized by law to discipline the physicians. The legislature gives the Board the authority to decide the punishment according to their full discretion from a fine up to revoking the license. If your license suspended or revoked, it is not easy for you to find the license in another state. The license suspension for years or revoking is equal or even worth than life sentence. The courts have not any practical control on the Board's Professional Judgment, and the Board and their order are immune against any level of the legal proceedings.

The Board of Medicine is physicians selected among the best physicians in the state. In the normal conditions, the Board acts are to protect the interest of Michigan People. The members of Board of Medicine are still human beings; they may do mistakes or wrongful acts. There is no authority or law or constitution above the Board of Medicine in their decision.

If the Board of Medicine intentionally targeted you and destroyed your assets and ruined your life and severely injured your patients without reason or for personal conflict or as retaliation for appealing their original order, where you go? You will be helpless no court can save you. **In this situations no difference if you are in the USA or North Korea.**

In 2010, People complained to the Board of Medicine for Dr. Farid Fata; Catholic Oncologist was giving chemotherapy for healthy patients and terminally ill hopeless cancer patients and committing fraud for money. The Board of Medicine dismissed all of the complaints until three years later the Federal Government arrested him for the same dismissed claims and sentenced him upon a guilty plea. On July 10, 2015, he was sentenced to 45 years in federal prison.

Because a retired nurse, cousin of administrative law judge works in the same agency, complained that I was giving her son narcotic while he was able to control his pain by Motrin, I was asked to pay $5000 fine. When I refused to pay the fine, so they suspended my License 6 months and $20,000 fine. Because I filed an appeal, they extended the suspension for unlimited years, and the Court of Appeals lost jurisdiction on the matter because it has no jurisdiction over the extension. Thousands of patients in critical condition, most of them officially considered disable, stable in my office for up to 10 years became medically homeless. The Board of Medicine was aware that this kind of patients could not secure their medicine and they are aware that the patients who on controlled medicine or addiction medicine are in risk of death if they could not secure their medicine on time.

Because of the absolute quasi-judicial immunity doctrine, I could not get help from any federal or state court.

The Board of Medicine guidelines of controlled medicine prescriptions state:

Physicians should not fear disciplinary action from the Board or other state regulatory or enforcement agency for prescribing, dispensing or administering controlled substances, including opioid analgesics, for a legitimate medical purpose and in the usual course of professional

> *practice. The Board will consider prescribing, ordering, administering or dispensing controlled substances for pain to be for a legitimate medical purpose if based on accepted scientific knowledge of the treatment of pain or if based on sound clinical grounds.*

On August 29th, 2013, Mr. Robert Regan, Registered Pharmacist, works as investigator at Licensing and Regulatory Affairs {LARA}, came to my office and stated that he was authorized by the Board of Medicine to investigate a complaint filed by mother of patient B.S. Later I learned that the mother is cousin of an administrative law judge, who conducted the administrative hearing, as he works in LARA as well.

The first question was whether I owned this office building and how much monthly rent I had been collecting from Pharmor Pharmacy, which was inside the building and he told me that do not allow Friendly Pharmacy put their flyers in my waiting room. He said: the mother of B.S. complained that I was giving her son narcotic while he was able to control his pain by Motrin. B.S. is an adult male, (DOB, 10/26/82), due to construction work accident, he has herniated spinal disc, spinal stenosis, chronic back pain, radiculopathy affecting the right leg, and anxiety. I told him that Motrin is not FDA approved for treating chronic back pain and I asked him whether a doctor recommended Motrin. He said no doctor, but his mother knew as she is a retired nurse. Treating the patient with chronic back pain due to structural spinal damage, spinal stenosis and radiculopathy with only Motrin as pain medicine for a long time is a criminal act.

On 9/16/2014, the Board of Medicine had filed an administrative complaint. The legislature required the board that the complaint about controlled medicine should be reviewed by a narcotic panel of 10 physicians before it was issued.

Michigan Legislature; MCL 333.16228:

(1) *For an investigation involving the prescription of a controlled substance, the department may establish an ad hoc review panel to provide the department with expert information regarding a specific health profession or health specialty or a specific health care treatment or procedure as it relates to the investigation. The department shall establish an ad hoc review panel under this subsection as follows:*
    (a) *The department shall triennially establish a pool of 10 physicians, 5 of whom are allopathic physicians licensed under part 170 and 5 of whom are osteopathic physicians licensed under part 175.*
    (b) *For each ad hoc review panel, the department shall appoint three physicians from the pool established under subdivision (a).*

(2) *The ad hoc review panel shall provide the information described in subsection (1) to the department during the investigation process and before a formal complaint is issued.*

The complaint was drafted by Bill Schuette, Michigan Attorney General and signed by Andrew Hudson, Assistant Attorney General {AAG} and it was on behalf of the Board of Medicine, Disciplinary Subcommittee. The narcotic panel did not review the complaint; even it was not reviewed by a nurse.

The complaint did not have the smell of medicine at all. The writer, through the complaint, was writing about Acetaminophen as the controlled medicine while it is the generic name of Tylenol, which is available for sale in the gas stations. I am going to show in the next chapters that nothing in the complaint has any legal value. When I responded to the complaint, I stated that the writer of the complaint did not belong to the medical field or he was committing fraud. Later on the administrative hearing, I had known that the writer of the complaint was Mr. Andrew Hudson, assistant attorney general. I think he might be graduated in the Law School about two years before writing this complaint. He was angry when he said to me: *"you know I wrote it as my name, who signed it."* He accused me that I was intentionally trying to defame him through talking about the defects in the complaint.

Mr. Hudson was not blamed for he did not know the basics of Medicine as he is a lawyer graduated from a Law School. He was blamed for writing a complaint in a critical branch of medicine from his knowledge without seeking help from a person belonging to the medical field such as a nurse.

The ALJ filed a proposal for decision (PFD) and I filed exceptions to PFD on time included indisputable evidence that all of the relevant facts were untrue and the result of perjury under oath. By law, the Board of Medicine acting as the final judge should review my exception and issue their final proposal for decision and final order.

The Board of Medicine had failed to review my exceptions in violation to the legislature. They adopted the PFD, which contains false facts; if a medical assistant read it, he would discover that it contains false facts and nothing in it justify any punishment. PFD and my exceptions to it are chapters 11 and 12.

I was Egyptian when I worked for seven years at King Faisal Hospital, Makah, Saudi Arabia. The Saudi do not have this kind of huge complicated executive and judicial systems, but if a lady complained about her son, the investigation and resolution of the issue would take few days to a week in the very simple proceeding. If there were judicial review, it would be directly in the matter, and it takes no more than few weeks. All stages of proceeding are before professionals experts in the subject. There was no chance for anyone to commit retaliation or do protected crimes and the interest of their patients is matter.

Here in America, I was facing ALJ's Proposal for Decision contains a fact stating that 10 mg Hydrocodone is equal to 750 mg Morphine, while ten is equal to 10 and Hydrocodone was DEA schedule III and Morphine DEA schedule II. The ALJ should not be blamed when he accused me of giving a high dose to his nephew because he was a judge, but the system should be blamed.

I had been fighting for years in multiple federal and state courts before people, attorney generals, and judges who are very far from the medical professions in a pure medical case. The courts are paralyzed by the absolute quasi-judicial immunity doctrine.

The issue could be resolved in few hours before a physician, who has experience in chronic pain management instead of hassling for years to decide if 10 mg Hydrocodone equal to 750 mg or 10 mg of Morphine as if it is Rocket Science.

CHAPTER 7

The Administrative Complaint

◆ ◆ ◆

Mr. Regan, a registered pharmacist, came to my office to investigate a complaint from a retired nurse about her son, who has a history of work accident caused herniated disc and spinal stenosis for I gave him narcotic while he was able to control his pain by Motrin. He was on narcotic before he came to my office and Motrin is not FDA approved for this kind of pain. Mr. Regan asked me if I own this office building and how much rent I was collecting from Pharmor Pharmacy and he asked me to do not allow Friendly Pharmacy put flyers in the waiting room.

On 9/18/2014, Mr. Hudson, AAG filed the next Administrative Complaint, I responded to it on time. Here next to the complaint, I am presenting few statements was quoted from my response to the complaint.

The STATE OF MICHIGAN
DEPARTMENT OF LICENSING AND REGULATORY AFFAIRS
BUREAU OF HEALTH CARE SERVICES
BOARD OF MEDICINE
DISCIPLINARY SUBCOMMITTEE

In the Matter of
ABDELBASET A. YOUSSEF, M.D.
License No. 43-01-081069
Complaint No. 43-12-126661
ADMINISTRATIVE COMPLAINT

Attorney General Bill Schuette, through Assistant Attorney General Andrew J. Hudson, on behalf of the Department of Licensing & Regulatory Affairs, Bureau of Health Care Services, (Complainant), files this complaint against Abdelbaset A. Youssef, M.D, (Respondent), alleging upon information and belief as follows:

1. *The Board of Medicine, (Board), an administrative agency established by the Public Health Code, (Code), 1978 PA 368, as amended, MCL 333.1101 et seq, is empowered to discipline licensees under the Code through its Disciplinary Subcommittee, (DSC).*
2. *Respondent is currently licensed to practice medicine pursuant to the Public Health Code.*
3. *APAP-Hydrocodone is a schedule 3 controlled substance.*
4. *Alprazolam (Xanax) is a schedule 4 controlled substance.*
5. *Promethazine with codeine is a schedule 5 controlled substance.*
6. *Carisoprodol (Soma) is a schedule 4 controlled substance.*
7. *Phentermine Hydrochloride is a schedule 4 controlled substance.*
8. *Zolpidem Tartrate (Ambien) is a schedule 4 controlled substance.*
9. *Lorazepam is a schedule 4 controlled substance.*
10. *Section 16221(a) of the Code provides the DSC with authority to take disciplinary action against Respondent for a violation of general duty, consisting of negligence or failure to exercise due care, including negligent delegation to, or supervision of employees or other individuals,*

whether or not injury results, or any conduct, practice, or condition which impairs, or may impairs, the ability to safely and skillfully practice medicine.

11. *Section 16621(b)(i) of the Code provides the DSC with authority to take disciplinary action against Respondent for incompetence, defined at section 16106(1) to mean a "departure from, or failure to conform to, minimal standards of acceptable and prevailing practice for a health profession whether or not actual injury to an individual occurs."*
12. *Section 16226 of the Code authorizes the DSC to impose sanctions against persons licensed by the Board if, after opportunity for a hearing, the DSC determines that a licensee violated one or more of the subdivisions contained in section 16221 of the Code.*

FACTS

General Allegations

13. *Based on data from the Michigan Automated Prescriptions System, Respondent prescribed 25,475 controlled substances between August 1, 2012, and July 31, 2013.*
14. *In an August 29, 2013, interview with a Bureau investigator, Respondent indicated that he sees patients five days per week. Therefore, Respondent prescribed an average of 102 prescriptions per day between August 1, 2012, and July 31, 2013.*
15. *The Bureau investigator reviewed Respondent's MAPS data and calculated that approximately 60% of his patients received the same three-drug combination of Hydrocodone, Alprazolam, and Carisoprodol. Respondent had no explanation for frequently prescribing this trio of narcotics.*

16. *The Bureau investigator obtained and reviewed several of Respondent's charts for patients receiving controlled substances. Respondent's charting shows a failure to follow the applicable standards practice in the following ways:*
    - A. *Failure to consider the use of other treatment modalities or non-narcotic medications for the treatment of pain.*
    - B. *Failure to consistently monitor for abuse and diversion by utilizing urine drug testing and checking patient's prescription records with MAPS.*
    - C. *Prescribing an inappropriate combination of medications.*
    - D. *Failure to appropriately assess and treat pain*
    - E. *Failure to document discussion with patients regarding the risks and benefits of narcotic treatment of pain*
    - F. *Failure to utilize and complete narcotic pain contracts, which delineate patient responsibilities and conditions under which treatment would be terminated.*

Patient B.S.

17. *Beginning in March 2011, Respondent treated patient B.S., an adult male, (d.o.b, 10/26/82), for chronic back pain, radiculopathy affecting the right leg, and anxiety. B.S. paid in cash only for his appointments.*
18. *MAPS data show that from March 2011 through October 2012, Respondent issued monthly prescriptions for APAP/Hydrocodone and Alprazolam to B.S. Beginning in May 2011, Respondent added prescriptions for promethazine with codeine to B.S.'s medication regimen.*
19. *Despite issuing prescriptions for three highly abused controlled substances, Respondent failed to obtain urine screens from B.S. or act*

upon MAPS data showing B.S. was obtaining APAP/Hydrocodone from multiple prescribers. Respondent failed to consider any other treatment modalities to address B.S.'s pain and anxiety. Respondent failed to appropriately document assessing B.S.'s pain or his progress toward goals of treatment.

20. *In October 2012, a family member of B.S. intervened when she noticed he was losing weight and was confrontational with others. Since leaving Respondent's care, the family member reported that B.S is managing his pain using mostly Motrin.*

<u>*Patient A.R.*</u>

21. *Beginning in September 2007, Respondent treated patient A.R., an adult female, (d.o.b, 04/27/72), for severe chronic neck and back pain due to a car accident many years ago. A.R. paid in cash only for her appointments.*
22. *MAPS data show that from October 2009 through November 2013, Respondent issued monthly prescriptions for APAP Hydrocodone, Alprazolam, and Phentermine Hydrochloride for A.R, Beginning in October 2011, Respondent added prescriptions for Zolpidem Tartrate and in November 2011, prescriptions for Promethazine with codeine to A.R.'s medication regimen.*
23. *Beginning in January 2012, Respondent added Carisoprodol to A.R.'s medication regimen.*
24. *Despite issuing prescriptions for the above combination of commonly abused controlled substances, Respondent did not document a narcotic pain contract with A.R. or document any discussion of the risks and benefits of such a combination of medications. Respondent failed to*

monitor A.R. for abuse or diversion of controlled substances through MAPS reports or urine drug screens.

25. *According to A.R.'s chart, Respondent failed to legibly document a recommendation of alternative treatment modalities for A.R. until April 2013.*

Patient C.H.

26. *Beginning in November 2009, Respondent treated patient C.H., an adult female, (d.o.b. 11/23/59), for chronic back and hip pain.*
27. *MAPS data show that before C.H. became Respondent's patient, she had filled prescriptions for 60 tablets of APAP/Hydrocodone at 500 mg on a monthly basis.*
28. *When C.H. became his patient, Respondent continued issuing prescriptions for APAP/Hydrocodone on a monthly basis, but he increased the dosage to 750 mg and increased the pill counts to 90 tablets. He also provided C.H. with monthly prescriptions for 46 tablets of alprazolam at 1 mg.*
29. *Beginning in January 2012, Respondent began issuing monthly prescriptions to C.H. for 60 tablets of Carisoprodol 350 mg.*
30. *Beginning in May 2012, Respondent began issuing monthly prescriptions to C.H. for 30 tablets of phentermine hydrochloride at 37.5 mg. Respondent failed to document any changes in C.H.'s weight during her regular office visits to verify the drug's effectiveness.*
31. *Beginning in June 2012, Respondent began issuing bi-annual prescriptions for codeine/promethazine.*
32. *Despite issuing prescriptions for the above inappropriate combination of commonly abused controlled substances, Respondent did not document*

any discussion of the risks and benefits of such a combination of medications. Respondent failed to monitor C.H. for abuse or diversion of controlled substances through MAPS reports or urine drug screens.

33. *Respondent failed to legibly document a recommendation of alternative treatment modalities for C.H. until April 2013.*

Patient K.B.

34. *Beginning in December 2008, Respondent treated patient K.B., an adult female, (d.o.b. 07/03/55), for chronic hip pain and Chronic Obstructive Pulmonary Disease.*
35. *Beginning in December 2008, MAPS data show that Respondent issued monthly prescriptions to K.B. for 120 tablets of APAP / Hydrocodone at 650 mg and 90 tablets of Lorazepam at 2 mg. At the same time, K.B obtained additional prescriptions, APAP / Hydrocodone and Lorazepam, from another provider. Respondent failed to monitor K.B. through MAPS reports to recognize her "doctor shopping."*
36. *Beginning in October 2009, Respondent began issuing monthly prescriptions for codeine/promethazine to K.B.*
37. *Beginning in January 2010, Respondent discontinued the prescriptions for Lorazepam and provided monthly prescriptions for 90 tablets of Alprazolam at 1 mg in its place. K.B. continued to obtain and fill prescriptions for Lorazepam from another provider.*
38. *Beginning in May 2011, Respondent began issuing bi-monthly prescriptions to K.B. for 30 tablets of phentermine hydrochloride at 37.5 mg. Respondent failed to document any changes in K.B.'s weight during her regular office visits and failed to document any alternative weight loss strategies.*

39. Despite issuing prescriptions for the above inappropriate combination of commonly abused controlled substances, Respondent did not document any discussion of the risks and benefits of such a combination of medications. Respondent failed to monitor K.B. for abuse or diversion of controlled substances through MAPS reports or urine drug screens.

40. Respondent failed to legibly document a recommendation of alternative treatment modalities for K.B. until April 2013

<u>COUNT I</u>

41. Respondent's conduct as described above constitutes negligence, in violation of section 16221(a) of the Code,

<u>COUNT II</u>

42. Respondent's conduct as described above constitutes incompetence, in violation of section 16221(b)(i) of the Code, THEREFORE, Complainant requests that this Complaint is served upon Respondent and that Respondent be offered an opportunity to show compliance with all lawful requirements for retention of the license above. If compliance is not shown, Complainant further requests that formal proceedings be commenced pursuant to the Public Health Code, rules promulgated pursuant to it, and the Administrative Procedures Act of 1969, 1969 PA 306, as amended; MCL 24,201 et seq; MSA 3,560(101) et seq.

RESPONDENT IS HEREBY NOTIFIED that, pursuant to section 16231(7) of the Public Health Code, Respondent has 30 days from the receipt of this Complaint to submit a written response to the allegations contained in it. The written response shall be submitted to the Bureau of Health Care Services, Department of Licensing and Regulatory Affairs, P.O. Box 30670, Lansing, Michigan, 48909, with a copy to the undersigned assistant attorney general. Further, pursuant to section 16231(8), failure to submit a written response within 30 days shall be treated as an admission of the allegations contained in the complaint and shall result in the transmittal of the complaint directly to the Board's Disciplinary Subcommittee for the imposition of an appropriate sanction.

Respectfully submitted,
BILL SCHUETTE Attorney General
Andrew J. Hudson (P76092)
Assistant Attorney General, Licensing & Regulation
P.O. Box 30758 Lansing, Michigan 48909
Dated: September 18, 2014 (517) 373-1146

Quoted from my response to the complaint

I responded to the complaint on time. The next is some paragraphs quoted from my response to the relevant allegations in the Administrative Complaint.

There are intentionally written misleading statements all over the complaint; for example, he said: *Beginning in May 2011, Respondent added prescriptions for promethazine with codeine to B.S.'s medication regimen.* I gave the patients this cough syrup about two times over the two years because he had a severe cough. He had the same cough medicine before he became my patient and after he left my office from other providers. Even after he left my office, he had two times cough medicine from another provider, but the dispensing pharmacist put them in my name on the MAPS. He had been writing the medications, by the way, to be understood as if I was giving all of the medications on the same visit.

Response to the allegation no. 13 is next:

Allegation no. 13, Based on data from the Michigan Automated Prescriptions System, Respondent prescribed 25,475 controlled substances between August 1, 2012, and July 31, 2013.

For the last ten years, I had been treating only patients with chronic pain syndrome along with the other medical problems, most of my patients were officially disable and most of them were my patients for about ten years. On average, each patient needed three controlled prescriptions per month or 36 prescriptions per year. I have more than 6000 charts in my office. The number of prescriptions is impossible to be evidence of negligence or incompetence.

In allegation no. 14, Mr. Hudsone stated: *Respondent had no explanation for frequently prescribing this trio of narcotics.*

Word trio of narcotics is clear evidence that the writer does not know the basics of medicine. Only one narcotic is in this trio; the other two are not narcotics.

Response to allegation no. 16 {a – f} is the next:

A – Failure to consider the use of other treatment modalities or non- narcotic medications for the treatment of pain:

Untrue! Every patient had at least one non-narcotic pain medicine beside one narcotic medicine. Mr. Hudson had known as he has copies of some patients' charts. Mr. Hudson did not know what the non-narcotic pain medicine was. Medicine that he talked about its dose changed from 500 mg to 750 mg is Tylenol, which is non-narcotic pain medicine. Every patient every visit had at least one non-narcotic pain medicine other than Tylenol.

B - Failure to consistently monitor for abuse and diversion by utilizing urine drug testing and checking patient's prescription records with MAPS.

Untrue! I had been doing MAPS every visit for all of my patients and Urine drug screen as needed. If otherwise, how my patients'

MAPS are 100% clean, some patients were my patients for more than ten years. MAPS is on the State website; Checking MAPS means reading it on the website. Moreover, Mr. Hudson saw pages printed from the MAPS website inside patient B.S.' chart. The ALJ documented that he read the MAPS reports in his Proposal for Decision (PFD), finding fact # 13, please read fact # 13; proposal for decision in chapter 12, in this book.

PFD finding fact # 13: *13. Prior to treating patient B.S., the Respondent obtained a report regarding patient B.S. from MAPS, [Testimony of Dr. Hopper; Petitioner's Exhibit D at pp. 1-41 to 1-42.]*

C - Prescribing an inappropriate combination of medications.

Untrue! All of the combinations were FDA approved and appropriate for the conditions of the patients. Mr. Hudson, AAG, Mr. Regan, Registered Pharmacist and mother of B.S. retired nurse are not qualified to comment on the issue of management of chronic pain syndrome. The even regular physician could not comment on this subject, so the legislature, MCL333.16228 requires a panel of 10 physicians to review the complaint in controlled medicine before its filing.

D - Failure to appropriately assess and treat pain.

Untrue! Patient N. M.: on 10/29/2013, I found the right diagnosis and saved her life after University of Michigan, and four other hospitals failed to diagnose her critical disease. The record is available at Oakwood Hospital Medical Center and E.R of the University of Michigan. Administrative Law Judge {ALJ} read the charts subject of this complaint, and he found the allegation was untrue he dismissed this allegation in his Proposal for Decision {PFD} Conclusion of Law. You may read the ALJ's PFD, in the next chapters.

E - Failure to document discussion with the patient regarding the risks and benefits of narcotic treatment of pain.

Untrue! The pain contract included in each chart signed by the patient had all of these details. On 10/29/2013, I succeeded to diagnose patient N.M., after the University of Michigan and other four Hospitals' E.R. failed to diagnose. The ALJ read the charts and dismissed this allegation in his proposal for decision; finding fact # 14 and his conclusion of Law. Pain contract is on the next page (Narcotic Prescription Authorization).

F - Failure to utilize and complete narcotic pain contracts, which delineate patient responsibilities and conditions under which treatment would be terminated.

Untrue! Every patient has pain contract in his chart, and the contract included all that complaint claimed and the Administrative Law Judge {ALJ} read the contracts and stated in his proposal for decision, that he read the contracts in the patients' charts and he dismissed these two allegations {e & f}as untrue. Please read PFD, chapter 10.

PFD fact no. 14: ***{14. On his first office visit with the Respondent, patient B.S. filled out a document entitled "Narcotic Prescription Authorization," which provided that patient B.S. would not "abuse, sell or share my medicine with another person" and that he would "seek narcotic prescription from only one physician or the emergency room during a specific time." Petitioner's Exhibit D at pp. 1-45}***

Next you; May find pain contract, stamp of Mr. Hudson in the end states that he presented it to be entered into evidence {126661 Attachment */W}

◆ ◆ ◆

Narcotic Prescription Authorization

I, B. S. , Born on *10/26/1982*

Authorize Astoria Medical Physicians to prescribe narcotics to relieve my severe pain. I acknowledge that narcotics may cause addiction and other serious side effects.

I hereby certify that I request narcotics only to relief my pain after the regular pain medicines are failed, intolerable and/or contraindicated, and request only the amount, I need and use it as prescribed for the same reason.

I acknowledge that Astoria Medical will not prescribe narcotics if they see that it is inappropriate medicine for me or the pain is not severe enough to receive this kind of medicine or the pain is manageable by another method.

I hereby certify that I will not abuse, sell or share my medicine with another person. I seek a narcotic prescription from only one physician or the emergency room during a specific time.

I acknowledge that Astoria Medical offer the appropriate amount of narcotics on handwritten prescriptions only with no refill, and they may not give me narcotics if they think that I abuse or receive the same medicine from other providers or I have not needed it anymore for pain relief.

I acknowledge that, if I lose my medicine or my prescription, Astoria Medical may not prescribe replacement.

Patient Signature ______________________ Date / / 20

Guardian Signature ____________________ Date / / 20

126661

ATTACHMENT * */-W*

◆ ◆ ◆

Next is from my response to allegations no. 19 and 20:

Allegation no. 20 – In October 2012, a family member of B.S. intervened when she noticed he was losing weight and was confrontational with others. Since leaving Respondent's care, the family member reported that B.S is managing his pain using mostly Motrin.

In response to allegation no. 19 and 20; B. S. took few times, a small amount of controlled pain medicine from the Emergency Room, he is allowed to do that, please read his pain contract on the previous page.

It is illegal to treat chronic back pain due to structural spinal injury and spinal stenosis by Motrin alone. Motrin is not FDA approved in this situation. I was giving a small amount of Motrin for inflammation. The analgesic equivalent of 10 mg of Hydrocodone is 2220 mg Motrin, which are 11 tablets of Motrin 200 mg. That the mother treated her son by Motrin without consulting physicians is a criminal act. Regarding that: She noticed her son losing weight, she stated in the hearing under oath that she asked her son: Why you look losing weight? He told her he did not eat well because his wife left his house, while he is taking care of 5 children from three women, and he has back pain.

In response to allegation no. *18 - MAPS data show that from March 2011 through October 2012, Respondent issued monthly prescriptions for APAP/ Hydrocodone and Alprazolam to B.S.*

The ALJ read B. S. chart and MAPS report and documented that patient B.S. was taking Hydrocodone from other physicians before he became my patient. Please read the proposal for decision {PFD] in this book finding fact # 16:

PFD finding fact no. 16; *16. According to the MAPS report, patient B.S. had previously been treated with Hydrocodone-containing products. [Petitioner's Exhibit E.1]*

Response to allegations no. 27 and 28:

Allegation no. 27- MAPS data show that before C.H. became Respondent's patient, she had filled prescriptions for 60 tablets of APAP/Hydrocodone at 500 mg on a monthly basis.

Allegation no. 28- When C.H. became his patient, Respondent continued issuing prescriptions for APAP/Hydrocodone on a monthly basis, but he increased the dosage to 750 mg and increased the pill counts to 90 tablets. He also provided C.H. with monthly prescriptions for 46 tablets of alprazolam at 1 mg.

In response to allegations no. 27 & 28; I stated: Mr. Hudson, the writer of the complaint, said that the patient before she became my patient she was taking Hydrocodone/APAP at 500, and after she became my patient I gave her Hydrocodone/APAP at 750. I changed her from Lortab 10/500 to Vicodin ES 7.5/750. I decreased the dose of Hydrocodone from 10 to 7.5 and increased the dose of Tylenol to 750 mg. The writer of the complaint did not know that the medicine he was talking about through the complaint was Tylenol. This act of negligence created personal conflict. Mr. Hudson controls all the business of the Board of Medicine as the Board members were busy in their medical practices far away; they just were visiting Lansing for few hour meeting every two months for drinking coffee and voting on the orders. So he had a chance to retaliate for he claimed that I was trying to defame him. He ruined my life and destroyed my assets and severely injured thousands of patients, using the name of the Board of Medicine as a tent.

In response to allegation no. 35, The patient took prescriptions from her Psychiatrist, only 2 or 3 times over eight years. She did that because of the medications, Xanax and Ativan, even belong to the same family of medicine, they did not have the same names. She was counseled and stopped to do that for five years. This condition is not a diversion, and it is not a crime. Law and my pain contract allow the patient may take controlled medicine from other providers in the state of emergency. Diversion means a patient who does doctors shopping to sell their medications.

Because in early 2009, I increased the dose of Tylenol for a patient, my License was suspended for years, and I lost my practice that my family and I had built over 13 years. Thousands of patients in critical conditions and on addiction treatment stable for up to 10 years found themselves in the streets, medically homeless.

If the Board of Medicine was not able to secure a panel of 10 physicians to review the complaint, as required by law, they should at least secure a nurse to review the complaint, but they did not do. The writer of the complaint stated in a hearing that the complaint was outside his experience. The complaint did not have any legal value.

CHAPTER 8

Felonies of the hearing

◆ ◆ ◆

I REFUSED TO PAY $5000 fine for settling the complaint because there was no cause for fine and I requested a schedule for hearing in the Administrative Hearing System. On 4/23/2015, the hearing was done before the Administrative Law Judge {ALJ} who was intentionally selected to be the cousin of the complainant, mother of patient B.S who was a witness in the hearing as well.

On 4/23/2015, during the hearing, everything is recorded in the transcript. Mr. Hudson gave me a stack of about 600 pages/papers and asked me to read and admit in 5 minutes. The ALJ entered the room and asked me if I admitted these papers, I told him I cannot admit; I do not know them. I need to read them at home. Even I stated that the ALJ stated that they were admitted. This stack of papers contained a report about three patients' charts, those patients were not my patients, and contained false information. The report was entered into evidence.

On 4/23/2015, during the hearing, the ALJ told Mr. Hudson, he noticed one of the witnesses was his cousin. Mr. Hudson said: yeas Judge, she is and he added; she is the complainant for her son, B.S. as well.

The mother of patient B.S. the complainant and the first witness stated that her son lost weight because he had trouble with his wife, who left home, and had five children from 3 women, has back pain, so he was not eating well. While the original Complaint stated that I was liable for his weight loss, the Proposal for Decision {PFD}, Fact no. 27, the ALJ considered me liable as well. She stated that he has a history of alcohol abuse and she found him drunk. She stated that she found two bottles of Vicodin and Atarax carrying my name, while I have not prescribed single tablet of these two medications, brand name or generic or under any name. Mr. Hudson knew, and he could not dispute, if I prescribed any of these medications, as they have B.S.' Chart and MAPS.

Witness, Mr. Robert Regan, R. Ph. Investigator and works for Licensing and Regulatory Affairs {LARA}: during the hearing, on 4/23/2015, he testified clear lies outside the scope of the allegations of the complaint to mislead the ALJ. Among his lies; he stated: because of respondent's patients in the market of Diversion, they have to go far to get the Pharmacy that dispenses their prescriptions, so they aggregate in pharmacies mostly far away, at Bellavista, Pharmor, Friendly, and Knight Drug Pharmacies.

The first Pharmacy was cross street from my office at 388 Inkster Rd, Inkster MI 48141. The second one was inside my office. When he came, he asked me how much rent I collect from it. The third one is close to my office so that he saw its flyers in the waiting room and asked me to stop that.

He said that I prescribe Hydrocodone, while Dr. Honet (Pain consultant) prescribes Morphine, while he knew Hydrocodone was DEA schedule III and Morphine was II. We were allowed to give five refills for Schedule III, in one visit, but no refill for Morphine. He tried to make the ALJ thinks Morphine is safer than Hydrocodone, as I was giving Hydrocodone to the ALJ's relative. All of these are lies outside the scope of the complaint added to the PFD.

Since Mr. Regan is a Pharmacist, I believed, he wrote the complaint, I asked him about the defects in the complaint. Mr. Hudson got angry and accused me that I knew that he, who wrote it as his name, who signed it. He accused me; I was trying to defame him. He stated: he did that because the subject of the complaint was outside his experience.

John Hopper, M.D., works for LARA as well and Expert witness: He was the expert witness in the hearing, on 4/23/2015. He was spraying lies without any restrictions. He testified lies not only in the subjects related to the complaint but also subjects not related to the complaint. He testified lies about patient A.R.'s Asthma and COPD. I filed Motion to the ALJ for his testimonies are lies and outside scope of the complaint. He filed report included three unknown patients, who were not my patients and the report contained lies.

He was not qualified to testify as expert witness in chronic pain management case, as he has never treated a single case of pain management in a primary care setting. I filed three motions to exempt him from being an expert witness and exempt his testimony and his report. My motions were denied for no clear reason.

Examples of his lies; he told the ALJ that: respondent was giving B.S. (ALJ's relative) 10 mg Hydrocodone, then 10 mg Hydrocodone is equal to 750 mg Morphine. Any textbook from Tokyo to New York says 10 mg Hydrocodone equal to 10 mg oral Morphine or 3.3 mg injectable Morphine. Another lie, the maximum dose of Xanax is 1 mg, while there are tablets of Xanax 3 mg. The maximum daily dose is 10 mg, could be more in case of emergency. Most of his testimonies were lies and outside the scope of the complaint.

The witnesses directed their grave lies about patient B.S, the ALJ's relative. They drew scenario as if I almost kill him. To make the ALJ loses his impartiality.

Many lies in the PFD, I answered them in my Exceptions to the PFD. I supported my answers in Exceptions with copies from three standard textbooks. Even I shipped the three textbooks to Mr. Hudson. I answered each fact and each conclusion of Law with indisputable evidence. Mr. Hudson has never disputed any of my evidence.

Even though I had known that Mr. Hudson conspired with Mr. Regan and Dr. Hopper to commit perjury in the hearing, I felt that there was hope to be corrected in the Board of Medicine, Disciplinary Subcommittee, because by Law, R 792.10131, they have to review my exceptions before the order became final,

R 792.10131. (3) A decision shall become a final decision in the absence of exceptions or review by an entity with final decision authority and MCL 333.16237(3) In reviewing the recommended findings of fact and conclusions of law of the hearings examiner and the record of the hearing, a disciplinary subcommittee may request the hearings examiner to take additional testimony or evidence on a specific issue or may revise the recommended findings of fact and conclusions of law as determined necessary by the disciplinary subcommittee, or both.

I was shocked by Dennis Szymanski, M.D., member of the Board of Medicine. He presented the final order for voting without reviewing my exceptions to the PFD as described by Laws. Even he did not mention them. Even if they did not review my exception or I did not file exceptions at all, there was nothing in the Proposal for Decision {PFD} justifying any punishment. Please read the PFD and my exceptions to the PFD in chapters: 11 and 12.

On 7/5/2016, in the second hearing, Mr. Hudson and Jessica Taub prepared and presented into evidence official documents contained forgery and presented a witness committed perjury.

I filed a motion to open the record and remove false documents. Jessica Taub practiced illegal pressure on and bribed my attorney to make me withdraw the motion. After she failed to respond to the motion, the ALJ returned the motion to protect here in violation of the Law.

The Board of Medicine voted for order extended the suspension from 6 months to years based on PFD stated what means that since I filed an appeal, the suspension should be extended. This retaliation was illegal.

CHAPTER 9

Hypocrisy of Michigan Legislature

◆ ◆ ◆

IN 1982, EGYPT IMPROVED THE Emergency Law. The old Emergency Law authorized the officer to arrest any person for any period. The amended Law authorized the officer to arrest any person, but the person can challenge the arrest in the court. The court should decide his arrest within 45 days. The maximum period of the illegal arrest became only 45 days, which was acceptable in a third world country. In practicing the Law, we found that thousands were arrested without cause for more than ten years because the Law did not set a limit for the number of arrests so that the officer would honor the court order and release the victim, but he would renew the arrest in the same page of the release. The amendment of the Law was functionless. It was better; it was not amended. It was not for use, but it was for the general public, who had never been arrested and for export outside the country, worldwide. Any person read the Law believes the illegal arrest is not more than 45 days, while in real life illegal arrest is for unlimited periods.

The third world and communist countries have many of hypocrisies in their Constitutions and Legislatures, which is not normal that you may find many of these hypocrisies in the civilized countries' legislatures. For example, Michigan Law: MCL333.16228, requires the

Board of Medicine before filing a complaint in controlled prescriptions, the complaint should be reviewed by ten physician controlled prescriptions panel.

MCL333.16228 Prescription of a controlled substance; investigation; ad hoc review panel.

(1) For an investigation involving the prescription of a controlled substance, the department may establish an ad hoc review panel to provide the department with expert information regarding a specific health profession or health specialty or a specific health care treatment or procedure as it relates to the investigation. The department shall establish an ad hoc review panel under this subsection as follows:

(a) The department shall triennially establish a pool of 10 physicians, 5 of whom are allopathic physicians licensed under part 170 and 5 of whom are osteopathic physicians licensed under part 175.

(b) For each ad hoc review panel, the department shall appoint three physicians from the pool established under subdivision (a).

(2) The ad hoc review panel shall provide the information described in subsection (1) to the department during the investigation process and before a formal complaint is issued.

When it came to the real life, the Board had filed a complaint against me, the writer of the complaint did not know even the basics in medicine, so he filed complaint vacant from any legal value, even he had been writing about Tylenol, as he believed it narcotic medicine. It was clear that even a nurse did not review it.

The more surprising was that the Court of Appeals stated that establishing the controlled prescription panel was optional as the statue said: {*the department may establish*}. So this Law is functionless, the Board of Medicine does not need it, it must be repealed. This Law gives false credibility for the complaint, as the general public and worldwide believes that each complaint was reviewed by ten physician panel, which is not reviewed by a nurse.

After the hearing in the Administrative Hearing System for a complaint, the Administrative Law Judge (ALJ) issue Proposal for Decision (PFD), contains facts and conclusion of law. The ALJ does not have the authority to issue the final order; he just works as a magistrate judge or referee. Within three weeks the physician may file an opposition to the PFD called Exceptions to the PFD. The Board of Medicine, Disciplinary Subcommittee shall review the PFD and the Exceptions to PFD and make its own PFD, and if they need further investigation, they may send the matter back to the ALJ, and they should issue the final order based on evidence as described by:

MCL333.16237. Imposition of penalty by disciplinary subcommittee; review of recommended findings of fact and conclusions of law; assignment of independent special assistant attorney general; additional testimony or evidence; sanction; completion of the action; appeal.

(1) *In imposing a penalty under section 16232(3), a disciplinary subcommittee shall review the recommended findings of fact and conclusions of law of the hearings examiner.*

(3) *In reviewing the recommended findings of fact and conclusions of law of the hearings examiner and the record of the hearing, a disciplinary subcommittee may request the hearings examiner to take additional testimony or evidence on a specific issue or may revise the recommended findings of fact and conclusions of law as determined necessary by the*

disciplinary subcommittee, or both. A disciplinary subcommittee shall not conduct its investigation or take its own additional testimony or evidence under this subsection.

(4) *If a disciplinary subcommittee finds that a preponderance of the evidence supports the recommended findings of fact and conclusions of law of the hearings examiner indicating that grounds exist for disciplinary action, the disciplinary subcommittee shall impose an appropriate sanction under any combination of this article, article 7, or article 8. If the disciplinary subcommittee finds that a preponderance of the evidence does not support the findings of fact and conclusions of law of the hearings examiner indicating that grounds exist for disciplinary action, the disciplinary subcommittee shall dismiss the complaint. A disciplinary subcommittee shall report final action taken by it in writing to the appropriate board or task force.*

After the ALJ filed the PFD, I filed Exceptions to the PFD included with indisputable evidence that all of the relevant findings of facts and conclusion of law were untrue and they were the result of perjury under oath and other violations. It was expected that the Board of Medicine reviews the Exceptions as described by law and asks the Michigan Attorney General may prosecute the culprits of perjury; instead, the Board of Medicine had failed to review the Exceptions. Even they did not mention the presence of the Exceptions in clear violation of the law.

The surprise was that the Michigan Court of Appeals stated that once the Board stated that they reviewed the record satisfies the requirement of MCL333.16237, even though they did not state specifically that they reviewed the Exceptions to the PFD.

Why did they tell me to file Exceptions if they are not required to review it? The MCL333.16237 with its long details is useless and should be repealed. The alternative statue shall not allow filling this functionless opposition. I am putting in the hands of the readers, the ALJ's Proposal for Decision and my Exceptions to PFD showing how the Hypocrisy of Michigan legal system tolerant to committing violations under the haven of the Law.

The final order suspension of the License for six months was subject to Judicial Review. Stay enforcement of the order was in the hand of the same person who issued it, who refused to stay it, while the Judicial Review took 18 months. Later the six-month suspension was extended to be for years and stated openly in an official document that, which means the extension, was retaliation for filing appeal. Judicial Review was punishment for the appellant, but it was not relief. The general public believes that the victim has a chance for Judicial Review which was not true. If they want to do a judicial review, they should stay the suspension pending appeal and protect the victim from retaliation and make the appeal within a reasonable period, and the Appellee should not be able to hijack the appeal before its deciding, such as by issuing secondary superseding orders practically removed the appeal from the Court.

MCL24.304(1) A petition shall be filed in the court within 60 days after the date of mailing notice of the final decision or order of the agency, or if a rehearing before the agency is timely requested, within 60 days after delivery or mailing notice of the decision or order thereon. The filing of the petition does not stay enforcement of the agency action, but the agency may grant, or the court may order, a stay upon appropriate terms.

While the original order suspension for six months was subject to pending Judicial Review, they issued new order extended the suspension to be for years. I filed a supplemental brief in the Court of Appeals may consider the new order along with the Original Order. The Court of Appeals had returned the brief for it had not had jurisdiction over the new order of the extension of suspension for years that supersedes the appealed order. So the pending appeal became moot or was hijacked before its deciding.

I had to take the new order to the Circuit Court first then it would come to the Court of Appeals in an extra season for more than two years. The Legislature should invalidate any order secondary or get its existence from the appealed order or at least keep jurisdiction in the same court. Michigan Legislature requires me to spend more than four years starving without work to review Mr. Hudson's order suspending my License for six months; it was issued due to personal conflict. The conflict was because Mr. Hudson saw that in 2009 I increased the dose of Tylenol for a patient. He considered addressing this defect a trial of defamation.

Next, you may read the Court of Appeals' order returned my supplemental brief for the Court had no jurisdiction on the new order that superseded the original order subject of the appeal so that the appeal was killed or hijacked before its deciding.

Court of Appeals, State of Michigan

ORDER

In re Abdelbaset Abdelmagid Youssef MD

Docket No. 330222 LC No. 15-015505

Michael F. Gadola, Judge, acting under MCR 7.211(E) (2) orders: 1 - The motion for immediate consideration of the motion to strike appellee's answer is GRANTED.

2 - The motion to strike appellee's answer is DENIED.

3 - The motion to file a supplemental brief filed on February 3, 2017, is DENIED. Thus, the Clerk's Office is directed to return the proposed second supplemental brief submitted with that motion to appellant without accepting it for filing.

The Court of Appeals' review stated that it was not their role to assess the credibility of the witness or proceeding in the hearing or the way by which the Board of Medicine is conducting a review of the exceptions. Once there was something called a hearing and the Board stated that they reviewed the record satisfy due process. My question is: what was supposed to be reviewed in the Court of Appeals? Why I went to the Court of Appeals in the first place?

The hypocrisy of the Legislature means writing a law that looks fine for general people at the same time it is a hell for the victims, so it is for export only. It is not for domestic use. It is to tell people worldwide that Americans have decent legislatures like Europe or any other civilized country. It is not for their people.

I worked as a Dermatologist in Saudi Arabia, which is a third world country and openly stated dictatorship, for seven years. They have perfect legal system regulates the medical professions. Physician investigates physician and nurse investigate nurse. They do not authorize a police officer to investigate or write a complaint against physicians in the medical subject. They do not tolerate or protect perjury in any level, and the law is respected. All felonies are illegal without exceptions. There is no doctrine legalizes the felonies, under any condition.

CHAPTER 10

Proposal for Decision

◆ ◆ ◆

NEXT IS THE ALJ'S PROPOSAL for Decision {PFD}, was issued by the Administrative Law Judge, the cousin of the complainant, mother of patient B.S., she was the first witness in the hearing, and the next chapter is my opposition to PFD, called Exceptions to the PFD. I defeated all of the relevant facts by indisputable evidence, included three textbooks.

THE STATE OF MICHIGAN

MICHIGAN ADMINISTRATIVE HEARING SYSTEM

Issued and entered this 18th day of June 2015
by Daniel L. Pulter, Administrative Law Judge
PROCEDURAL HISTORY

This matter was brought under the Michigan Public Health Code (Code), 1978 PA 368, as amended, MCL 333.1101 *et seq.*, and concerns an Administrative Complaint issued on September 18, 2014, brought by the Bureau of Health Care Services (Petitioner) against the physician's license of Abdelbaset Abdelmagid Youssef, M.D. (Respondent).

On March 16, 2015, the Michigan Administrative Hearing System issued a Notice of Hearing, scheduling a contested case hearing for April 23, 2015. Prior to the hearing, the Respondent filed on April 1, 2015, a motion for summary disposition for failure to state a claim upon which relief can be granted. An Order denying such Motion was filed on April 7, 2015. The hearing was held as scheduled on April 23, 2015.

Andrew J. Hudson, Assistant Attorney General, appeared on behalf of the Petitioner; and the Respondent appeared *in propria persona.* The Petitioner called Candice L. Suydam, RN; Robert Regan, R. Ph.; and John A. Hopper, M.D., to testify as witnesses. The following exhibits were offered by the Petitioner and admitted into the record as evidence:

The record in this matter was closed at the conclusion of the hearing on April 23, 2015. Subsequent to closing the record, the Respondent has filed four motions regarding a re-opening of the record. The first Motion, dated April 23, 2015, sought to re-open the record for the purpose of striking part of the testimony of Dr. Hopper. The second Motion, dated April 26, 2015, sought the re-opening of the record for the purpose of presenting evidence of treatment of patients other than those referenced in the Administrative Complaint. On May 11, 2015, this Tribunal issued an Order denying the first and second Motions. Thereafter, in the third Motion, dated May 14, 2014, the Respondent again seeks to re-open the record for the purpose of setting aside the expert report of Dr. Hopper. In the fourth Motion, dated May 16, 2014, the Respondent seeks to re-open the record for the purpose of attacking the credentials of Dr. Hopper, as an expert witness. The Order denying the third and fourth Motions is filed contemporaneous with this Proposal for Decision and is incorporated by reference herein.

ISSUES AND APPLICABLE LAW

As alleged in Counts I and II of the Administrative Complaint dated September 18, 2014, the issues presented in this matter are whether Respondent has violated Section 16221(a) and Section 16221(b)(i).

FINDINGS OF FACT

Based on the entire record in this matter, including the witness testimony and admitted exhibits, the following findings of fact are established:

1. At all times relevant to the Administrative Complaint, the Respondent was licensed as a physician in the State of Michigan and had an office in Wayne, Michigan; [Testimony of the Respondent.]
2. At all times relevant to the Administrative Complaint, the Respondent's medical practice involved pain management; [Testimony of Dr. Hopper; Testimony of the Respondent.]
3. According to the Drug Abuse Warning Network and the Drug Enforcement Agency, the following five narcotic medications are high-profile in the drug divergent market: Promethazine with Codeine, Alprazolam, Carisoprodol, Hydrocodone, and Oxycodone; [Testimony of Mr. Regan.]
4. For the period from August 1, 2012, through July 31, 2013, the Respondent issued repetitive prescriptions for four of the top five divergent drugs, being Promethazine with Codeine, Alprazolam, Carisoprodol, and Hydrocodone, which amounted

to 86 percent of the prescriptions issued by the Respondent, [Testimony of Mr. Regan; Petitioner's Exhibit B at p. 2.]

5. The Respondent issued 25,475 prescriptions for controlled substances during the one-year period from August 1, 2012, through July 31, 2013. [Testimony of Mr. Regan; Petitioner's Exhibit B.1
6. Based on a five-day work week, or 250 working days per year, the Respondent issued, on the average, 102 controlled substance prescriptions per day during the one-year period from August 1, 2012, through July 31, 2013. [Testimony of Mr. Regan; Petitioner's Exhibit B.1]
7. When a patient is in the drug diversion business, the patient will have difficulty finding a pharmacy to dispense the prescription, because pharmacists have a responsibility to ensure that prescriptions are for legitimate medical needs; [Testimony of Mr. Regan.]
8. When patients in the drug diversion business locate a pharmacy that will dispense the prescriptions, a large number of such patients will congregate to such pharmacies to have their controlled substances dispensed; [Testimony of Mr. Regan.]
9. There are five pharmacies where the Respondent's patients frequently fill their prescriptions, being Bellavista Pharmacy, Knight Drugs-Grand Blanc, Pharmor Pharmacy-Alien Park, and Friendly Pharmacy, some of which are located a great distance from the Respondent's office. [Testimony of Mr. Regan; Petitioner's Exhibit B at p. 3.]
10. Dr. Honet, a board-certified pain management specialist, issued 13,096 prescriptions for controlled substances over the

twelve month period from January 1, 2012, through December 31, 2012. [Testimony of Mr. Regan; Petitioner's Exhibit C.1

11. The most prescribed controlled substance by Dr. Honet is Morphine, while the most prescribed controlled substance by the Respondent is Hydrocodone. [Testimony of Mr. Regan; Petitioner's Exhibit B: Petitioner's Exhibit C.1]
12. Patient B.S. is a 32-year-old male, who has a herniated disc in his back and suffers from back pain; [Testimony of Nurse Suydam; Petitioner's Exhibit D at pp. 1-43.]
13. Prior to treating patient B.S., the Respondent obtained a report regarding patient B.S. from MAPS; [Testimony of Dr. Hopper; Petitioner's Exhibit D at pp. 1-41 to 1-42.]
14. On his first office visit with the Respondent, patient B.S. filled out a document entitled "Narcotic Prescription Authorization," which provided that patient B.S. would not "abuse, sell or share my medicine with another person" and that he would "seek narcotic prescription from only one physician or the emergency room during a specific time." Petitioner's Exhibit D at pp. 1-45.]
15. On his first office visit with patient B.S., the Respondent prescribed a 10 mg dose of Hydrocodone for patient B.S. [Testimony of Dr. Hopper; Petitioner's Exhibit E, at p. 2.]
16. According to the MAPS report, patient B.S. had previously been treated with Hydrocodone-containing products. [Petitioner's Exhibit E.1
17. **Ten mg of Hydrocodone is equivalent to 750 mg of Morphine; [Testimony of Dr. Hopper.]**
18. On his first office visit with patient B.S., the Respondent also prescribed a 1 mg dose of Alprazolam, which is a controlled

substance that had not been previously prescribed to patient B.S. [Testimony of Dr. Hopper; Petitioner's Exhibit E, at p. 2.]

19. **A 1 mg dose of Alprazolam is the most potent dosage of the medication; [Testimony of Dr. Hopper.]**
20. An appropriate starting dose of Alprazolam is 0.25 mg. [Testimony of John A. Hopper, M.D.]
21. The prescription of Alprazolam was issued to patient B.S. with no prior medical records other than a magnetic resonance imaging report of patient B.S.'s back. [Testimony of Dr. Hopper; Petitioner's Exhibit D]
22. There is no indication that any non-medication therapies were used for treatment of pain for patient B.S. [Testimony of Nurse Suydam; Testimony of Dr. Hopper; Petitioner's Exhibit D.1
23. There is no indication that the Respondent tried to set and assess functional goals, or attempted any referrals for physical therapy or rehabilitation for patient B.S. [Testimony of Candice L. Suydam, R.N.; Testimony of John A. Hopper, M.D.; Petitioner's Exhibit D.1
24. According to MAPS, patient B.S. obtained a prescription for Diazepam from a physician other than Respondent in August 2012. [Petitioner's Exhibit E.1]
25. According to MAPS, the Respondent prescribed Hydrocodone, Promethazine with Codeine, Carisoprodol, and Alprazolam for patient B.S. in September and October 2012. [Petitioner's Exhibit E.1]
26. There is no evidence from the record that the Respondent ran a MAPS report prior to issuing any prescriptions to patient B.S. in September and October 2012; [Petitioner's Exhibit D.1]

27. In October 2012, Nurse Suydam noticed that her son, patient B.S., had lost weight; [Testimony of Nurse Suydam.]
28. In October 2012, Nurse Suydam found patient B.S. sitting on the floor of his house, leaning against the wall with vacant eyes; [Testimony of Nurse Suydam.]
29. When Nurse Suydam found him in his house, patient B.S. was slow to respond to her questioning; [Testimony of Nurse Suydam.]
30. At that time, Nurse Suydam found various prescription medications in patient B.S.'s house; [Testimony of Nurse Suydam.]
31. Nurse Suydam believed that patient B.S. had overdosed on a combination of medications. [Testimony of Nurse Suydam]
32. Patient B.S. was admitted into a drug rehabilitation center at Washington Way Recovery Center in Jackson, Michigan; [Testimony of Nurse Suydam.]
33. Upon completion of treatment for drug addiction, patient B.S. is still struggling with back pain, but he now manages his pain with Motrin; [Testimony of Nurse Suydam.]
34. Patient A.R. is a 43-year-old female, who has a herniated disc in her back and suffers from back pain. [Petitioner's Exhibit F at pp. 5-164].
35. Patient A.R. reported "10 out of 10" pain over the course of her six-year treatment by the Respondent. [Testimony of Dr. Hopper; Petitioner's Exhibit F.1
36. In patient A.R.'s records covering a six-year period, there is no indication that the Respondent used any non-medication therapies for the treatment of patient A. R.'s pain. [Testimony of Dr. Hopper; Petitioner's Exhibit F: Petitioner's Exhibit M.1

37. Although patient A.R. was reporting "10 out of 10" pain, there is no indication from patient A.R.'s records that the Respondent made any change to the treatment plan for patient A.R., other than continue to prescribe a combination of controlled substances. [Testimony of Dr. Hopper; Petitioner's Exhibit F: Petitioner's Exhibit M.1
38. In patient A.R.'s records covering a six-year period, there is no indication that the Respondent tried to set and assess functional goals or attempted any other referrals such as physical therapy, rehabilitation, or pain specialists. [Testimony of Dr. Hopper; Petitioner's Exhibit F: Petitioner's Exhibit M.1
39. There is no evidence in patient A.R.'s medical records that the Respondent ever reviewed MAPS or conducted a urine drug screen of patient A.R. to monitor her usage of the controlled substances. [Testimony of Dr. Hopper; Petitioner's Exhibit F: Petitioner's Exhibit M.1
40. In August 2013, the Respondent prescribed Hydrocodone, Alprazolam, Carisoprodol, Temazepam, Tramadol, and Phentermine for patient A.R. [Petitioner's Exhibit F: Petitioner's Exhibit G: Respondent's Exhibit M.1
41. Along with the foregoing medications, the Respondent also prescribed Zolpidem Tartrate for patient A.R. in March 2013. [Petitioner's Exhibit G; Respondent's Exhibit M.1
42. Along with the foregoing medications, the Respondent also prescribed Promethazine with Codeine for patient A.R. in October 2012. [Petitioner's Exhibit G: Respondent's Exhibit M.1
43. There was nothing in the Respondent's records to indicate any monitoring of patient A.R. by the Respondent. [Testimony of John A. Hopper, M.D.; Petitioner's Exhibit M.1

44. The combination of the medications prescribed by the Respondent for patient A.R. is very risky in terms of sedation and multiple potential for interactions. [Testimony of Dr. Hopper; Petitioner's Exhibit G: Petitioner's Exhibit M at p. 4.]
45. The combination of medications prescribed by the Respondent for patient A.R. is sedative with potential overdose risk alone or in combination; [Testimony of Dr. Hopper; Petitioner's Exhibit M at p. 4.]
46. Although the Respondent treated patient A.R. for ten years, Petitioner's Exhibit F contains only six years of the Respondent's patient records for patient A.R. [Petitioner's Exhibit M at p. 4.]
47. Patient C.H. is a 56-year-old female, who has herniated discs and bulging discs in her back, and suffers from spinal stenosis and back pain; [Petitioner's Exhibit H, at pp. 7-1 and 7-84 to 7-91.]
48. With respect to patient C.H., there is no evidence of any modalities for pain, other than prescribing of medications. [Testimony of Dr. Hopper; Petitioner's Exhibit H: Petitioner's Exhibit M. l
49. There was no evidence of an assessment of function for patient C.H., or any referral by the Respondent for other treatments for chronic pain. [Testimony of Dr. Hopper; Petitioner's Exhibit H: Petitioner's Exhibit: M. l]
50. There is no evidence in patient C.H.'s medical records that the Respondent ever reviewed MAPS or conducted a urine drug screen, or used any other method to monitor patient C.H.'s usage of controlled substances. [Testimony of Dr. Hopper; Petitioner's Exhibit H: Petitioner's Exhibit M. l

51. Since 2009, the Respondent has consistently prescribed Hydrocodone and Alprazolam for patient C.H. [Petitioner's Exhibit 1.1
52. Phentermine was added as a prescription for patient C.H. in July 2010. [Petitioner's Exhibit 1.1
53. Carisoprodol was added as a prescription for patient C.H. in January 2011, and there was no documentation regarding why this controlled substance was added for treatment of patient C.H. [Testimony of Dr. Hopper; Petitioner's Exhibit M at p. 5.]
54. The Respondent also prescribed Promethazine with Codeine for patient C.H. in June, October, and December 2012, and in May 2013. Petitioner's Exhibit 1.1
55. The documentation does not support the combination of controlled substances prescribed for patient C.H. by the Respondent; [Testimony of Dr. Hopper; Petitioner's Exhibit M at p. 6.]
56. The combination of medications prescribed by the Respondent for patient C.H. had the potential for worsening her hypertension; [Testimony of Dr. Hopper; Petitioner's Exhibit M at p. 6.]
57. Patient K.B. is a female of undisclosed age, who according to the Respondent's records suffers from back pain and hip pain. [Petitioner's Exhibit J at pp. 11-109 to 11-111.]
58. There was no evidence in patient K.B.'s medical records of non-medication treatments for patient K.B.'s pain. [Testimony of Dr. Hopper; Petitioner's Exhibit J: Petitioner's Exhibit M at p. 8.]

59. There was no evidence in patient K.B.'s medical records that the Respondent had assessed patient K.B.'s level of function to determine if she was improving based on function. [Testimony of Dr. Hopper; Petitioner's Exhibit J: Petitioner's Exhibit M at p. 8.]
60. There is no evidence in patient K.B.'s medical records that the Respondent ever reviewed MAPS or conducted a urine drug screen, or used any other method to monitor patient K.B.'s usage of controlled substances; [Testimony of Dr. Hopper; Petitioner's Exhibit J: Petitioner's Exhibit M. l]
61. According to MAPS, patient K.B. obtained prescriptions for Hydrocodone and Lorazepam from a physician other than the Respondent in February, August, and October 2011. [Petitioner's Exhibit E.1]
62. According to MAPS, the Respondent also prescribed Hydrocodone and Lorazepam for patient K.B. in February, August, and October 2011. [Petitioner's Exhibit E.1
63. The Respondent prescribed Hydrocodone, Alprazolam, Promethazine with Codeine, Lorazepam, Phentermine, Butalbital, and Carisoprodol for patient K.B.; [Testimony of Dr. Hopper; Petitioner's Exhibit K.1].
64. The combination of controlled substances prescribed by the Respondent for patient K.B. could cause sedation, confusion and death; [Testimony of Dr. Hopper.]
65. There is no documentation in the Respondent's patient records of any discussion regarding the risks and benefits of using controlled substances in the treatment of obesity; [Petitioner's Exhibit M at p. 8.]

66. A minimal standard of acceptable practice for a physician is that a physician should explore other treatment modalities when dealing with a patient with chronic pain, such as considering referrals; [Testimony of Dr. Hopper.]
67. A minimum standard of acceptable practice for a physician administering pain medication is to assess a patient's level of function to determine if the patient is improving based on function; [Testimony of Dr. Hopper.]
68. The goal of physical therapy is improved function, not pain management; [Testimony of Dr. Hopper.]
69. There is no empirical evidence that medication improves function; [Testimony of Dr. Hopper.]
70. Even if a patient refuses physical therapy; it does not indicate that a controlled substance should be used, but if it is prescribed, appropriate documentation of the refusal of physical therapy should be included in the patient records; [Testimony of Dr. Hopper.]
71. Long-term use of regular muscle relaxants probably does not improve function; [Testimony of Dr. Hopper.]
72. A minimal standard of care for a physician requires the monitoring of patients who have been prescribed controlled substances. [Testimony of Dr. Hopper; Petitioner's Exhibit M at p. 4.]
73. Physicians should employ a variety of techniques to prevent their patients from diverting controlled substances, including obtaining a MAPS report, not prescribing controlled substances or starting at low doses of controlled substances, requiring urine testing, performing pill counts, and also being aware of patients who have risks for addictions, such as cigarette smokers or men who have a history of drug or alcohol use; [Testimony of Dr. Hopper.]

74. A minimal standard of acceptable practice for a physician is that the physician will inquire about the use of other controlled substances prescribed for the patient by other physicians; [Testimony of Dr. Hopper.]
75. The combination of Hydrocodone and Alprazolam, in general, probably worsens patients more than getting one of these drugs alone; [Testimony of Dr. Hopper.]
76. Based on his patient records, the Respondent is treating chronic pain with controlled substances, and is also treating the secondary effects of the chronic pain, anxiety, with additional controlled substances; [Testimony of Dr. Hopper.]
77. A minimum standard of acceptable practice for a physician in treating a patient who has anxiety related to pain is to treat the patient's pain, not to treat the patient with anxiety medication; [Testimony of Dr. Hopper.]
78. A minimum standard of acceptable practice for a physician would require, before prescribing an anxiety medication, to take appropriate medical history, arrive at a reasonable differential diagnosis, start treatment based on the physician's suspicions, and follow up and monitor the patient; [Testimony of Dr. Hopper.]
79. The first line treatment for anxiety is non-controlled substances, including selective serotonin reuptake inhibitors (SSRIs), such as Prozac and Paxil, or a second line treatment of serotonin-norepinephrine reuptake inhibitors (SNRIs), which could treat pain and depression; [Testimony of Dr. Hopper.]
80. While Alprazolam may be prescribed for the treatment of anxiety, a patient who has anxiety from pain should be treated to relieve the pain; [Testimony of Dr. Hopper.]

81. There was no evidence contained in the Respondent's patient records supporting the prescribing of Alprazolam to treat anxiety caused by chronic pain; [Testimony of Dr. Hopper.]
82. Carisoprodol is not an appropriate muscle relaxant for chronic use; [Testimony of Dr. Hopper.]
83. Carisoprodol is a very dangerous drug, which can produce physical dependence and seizures if the prescription is stopped suddenly; [Testimony of Dr. Hopper.]
84. While Carisoprodol is used as a muscle relaxant, there are five cheaper, safer muscle relaxants that can be used; [Testimony of Dr. Hopper.]
85. The pain suffered by a patient who has chronic pain syndrome can be treated by one or more controlled substances; [Testimony of Dr. Hopper.]

Conclusions of Law

Petitioner, as the complaining party in this matter, has the burden of proof to show by a preponderance of the evidence that Respondent has violated the Code provisions as set forth in Counts I and II of the Administrative Complaint, such that grounds exist for the imposition of a sanction or sanctions R 792.10707(1). As the Michigan Supreme Court has stated, "[p]roof by a preponderance of the evidence requires that the fact finder believe that the evidence supporting the existence of the contested fact outweighs the evidence supporting its nonexistence." *Blue Cross & Blue Shield of Michigan v Milliken,* 422 Mich. 1, 89; 367 NW2d 1 (1985).

In Count I of the Administrative Complaint, the Petitioner alleged that the Respondent violated Section 16221(a), which entails "[a] violation of general duty consists of negligence or failure to exercise due care" MCL 333.16221(a). In Count II of the Administrative Complaint, the Petitioner alleged that the Respondent violated Section 16221(b)(i), which requires proof of "incompetence," which is defined as "a departure from, or failure to conform to, minimal standards of acceptable and prevailing practice for a health profession, whether or not actual injury to an individual occurs" MCL 333.16106 (1).

In the Administrative Complaint, the following allegations are alleged as the basis for violations of Sections 16221(a) and 16221 (b)(i): (a) Failure to consider the use of other treatment modalities or non-narcotic medications for the treatment of pain; (b) Failure to consistently monitor for abuse and diversion by utilizing urine drug testing and checking patients' prescription records with MAPS; (c) Prescribing an inappropriate combination of medications; (d) Failure to appropriately assess and treat pain; (e) Failure to document discussion with patients regarding the risks and benefits of narcotic treatment of pain; and (f) Failure to utilize the complete narcotic pain contracts, which delineate patient responsibilities and conditions under which treatment would be terminated. Each of these alleged violations will be separately addressed below.

A - Failure to consider the use of other treatment modalities or non-narcotic medications for the treatment of pain.

Based on the above Findings of Fact, the Petitioner has shown by a preponderance of the evidence that the Respondent did not employ any non-medication therapies for the treatment of pain for patient B.S., patient A.R., patient C.H. and patient K.B. Also, there is no indication from the Respondent's patient records that he tried to set and assess functional goals, or attempted any referrals for physical therapy or rehabilitation for patient B.S., patient A.R., patient C.H., and patient K.B. Dr. Hopper credibly testified that a minimal standard of acceptable practice for a physician is that a physician should explore other treatment modalities when dealing with a patient with chronic pain.

Based on the Findings of Fact, the Petitioner has met its burden of proof concerning the Respondent's failure to consider the use of other treatment modalities or non-narcotic medications for the treatment of pain. It is concluded that the Respondent's failure to consider the use of other treatment modalities or non-narcotic medications for the treatment of pain constitutes a violation of general duty, consisting of a failure to exercise due care MCL333.16221 (a). Moreover, it is concluded that the Respondent's failure to consider the use of other treatment modalities or non-narcotic medications for the patients.

While it is clear that the allegations of the Administrative Complaint challenged the Respondent's treatment for chronic pain, significant testimony was received regarding the Respondent's treatment of other conditions, such as Asthma, Chronic Obstructive Pulmonary Disease, and Obesity. Inasmuch as such testimony was outside of the allegations of the Administrative Complaint, only the allegations of the Administrative Complaint will be addressed herein treatment of pain constitutes incompetence, or a departure from, or failure to conform to minimal standards of acceptable and prevailing practice for a health profession. MCL 333.16221 (b) (i); MCL 333.16106(1).

B - Failure to consistently monitor for abuse and diversion by utilizing urine drug testing and checking patients' prescription records with MAPS.

Based on the Findings of Fact, the Petitioner has shown by a preponderance of the evidence that the Respondent was not monitoring his patients for abuse and diversion by utilizing urine drug screening or by obtaining periodic MAPS reports for such patients. In fact, the record contains at least one example of abuse or diversion. During the time the Respondent had prescribed controlled substances for patient K.B., she obtained duplicate controlled substances from another physician. This duplication of prescriptions could have been avoided if the Respondent had performed a review of MAPs prior to issuing prescriptions for controlled substances to patient K.B. Dr. Hopper credibly testified that a minimal standard of care for a physician requires monitoring of patients who have been prescribed controlled substances.

Based upon the Findings of Fact, the Petitioner has met its burden of proof concerning the Respondent's failure to consistently monitor for abuse and diversion by utilizing urine drug testing and checking patient's prescription records with MAPS. It is concluded that the Respondent's failure to consistently monitor for abuse and diversion by utilizing urine drug testing and checking patient's prescription records with MAPS constitutes a violation of general duty, consisting of a failure to exercise due care. MCL 333.16221(a). Moreover, it is concluded that the Respondent's failure to consistently monitor for abuse and diversion by utilizing urine drug testing and checking patient's prescription records with MAPS constitutes incompetence, or a departure from, or failure to conform to minimal standards of acceptable and prevailing practice for a health profession. MCL 333.16221 (b)(i); MCL 333.16106(1).

C - Prescribing an inappropriate combination of medications.

Based on the Findings of Fact, the Petitioner has shown by a preponderance of the evidence that the Respondent prescribed an inappropriate combination of medications. The Respondent treated patient

B.S., patient A.R., patient C.H., and patient K.B. with Hydrocodone, Alprazolam, Carisoprodol, and Promethazine with Codeine. The Respondent treated his patients with Alprazolam for anxiety caused by chronic pain, without first attempting to treat such anxiety with non-controlled substances, such as SSRIs and SNRIs. The Respondent treated his patients with Carisoprodol used as a muscle relaxant, instead of one of the five cheaper, safer muscle relaxants that can be used. The Respondent was treated his patients with higher doses of the controlled substances, instead of starting at lower doses.

Based on the Findings of Fact, the Petitioner has met its burden of proof concerning the Respondent's prescribing of an inappropriate combination of medications. It is concluded that the Respondent's prescribing of an inappropriate combination of medications constitutes a violation of general duty, consisting of a failure to exercise due care MCL333.16221 (a). Moreover, it is concluded that the Respondent's prescribing of an inappropriate combination of medications constitutes incompetence, or a departure from, or failure to conform to minimal standards of acceptable and prevailing practice for a health profession. MCL 333.16221 (b)(i); MCL 333.16106(1).

D - Failure to appropriately assess and treat pain.

The Findings of Fact indicate that the Respondent has assessed pain in patient B.S., patient A.R., patient C.H., and patient K.B. The record is also clear that the Respondent treated such pain with various controlled substances. Dr. Hopper credibly testified that the pain suffered by a patient who has chronic pain syndrome could be treated by one or more controlled substances. From such Findings of Fact, it is clear that the Respondent has assessed and treated pain in patient B.S., patient

A.R., patient C.H., and patient K.B. The Petitioner's real objection to the Respondent's treatment of patient B.S., patient A.R., patient C.H., and patient K.B. is the fact that the Respondent did not consider the use of other treatment modalities or non-narcotic medications for the treatment of pain, which is a separate alleged violation of the Code addressed above.

Based on the Findings of Fact, the Petitioner has failed to demonstrate, by a preponderance of the evidence, that the Respondent violated the Code by the failure to appropriately assess and treat pain. Therefore, based upon the Findings of Fact, it is concluded there was no violation of general duty, consisting of a failure to exercise due care, MCL 333.16221 (a), and there was no departure from or failure to conform to minimal standards of acceptable and prevailing practice for a health profession. MCL 333.16221 (b)(i); MCL 333.16106(1).

E - Failure to document discussion with the patient regarding the risks and benefits of narcotic treatment of pain.

Other than the allegations of the Administrative Complaint, the Petitioner failed to support this allegation with any testimony or documentary evidence at the hearing with respect to patient B.S., patient A.R., and patient C.H. With respect to patient K.B., the expert report of Dr. Hopper indicated that there is no documentation in the Respondent's patient records of any discussion regarding the risks and benefits of using controlled substances in the treatment of obesity. [Petitioner's Exhibit M at p. 8.] However, the Petitioner failed to elicit any testimony as to the minimum standards of acceptable and prevailing practice for a physician concerning patient discussions regarding the risks and benefits of narcotic treatment of pain. Based on these Findings of Fact, the Petitioner has failed to demonstrate, by a preponderance of the evidence, that the Respondent violated the Code by the failure to document discussion with the patient regarding the risks and benefits of narcotic treatment of pain. Therefore, based upon the Findings of Fact, it is concluded there was no violation of general duty, consisting of a failure to exercise due care, MCL 333.16221(a), and there was no departure from or failure to conform to minimal standards of acceptable and prevailing practice for a health profession. MCL 333.16221 (b)(i); MCL 333.16106(1).

F - Failure to utilize and complete narcotic pain contracts, which delineate patient responsibilities and conditions under which treatment would be terminated.
Other than the allegations of the Administrative Complaint, the Petitioner failed to support this allegation with any testimony at the hearing. According to the documentary evidence, in this case, the patient records which were admitted into the record constitute only a fraction of the Respondent's patient records. As noted in the Findings of Fact, the Respondent treated patient A.R. for ten years, although Petitioner's Exhibit F contains only six years of the Respondent's patient records for patient A.R. The Petitioner has thus failed in its proofs to demonstrate that, more likely than not, no such narcotic pain contract is contained in patient A.R.'s records. As demonstrated in the Findings of Fact, patient B.S.'s medical records contain a document entitled "Narcotic Prescription Authorization" which could be construed to be a narcotic pain contract, [See, e.g., Petitioner's Exhibit D at pp. 1-45.] This document recites that patient B.S. would not "abuse, sell or share

my medicine with another person" and that he would "seek a narcotic prescription from only one physician or the emergency room during a specific time." id.

Based on the Findings of Fact, the Petitioner has failed to demonstrate, by a preponderance of the evidence, that the Respondent violated the Code by the failure to utilize and complete narcotic pain contracts, which delineate patient responsibilities and conditions under which treatment would be terminated. Therefore, based upon the Findings of Fact, it is concluded there was no violation of general duty, consisting of a failure to exercise due care, MCL 333.16221(a), and there was no departure from or failure to conform to minimal standards of acceptable and prevailing practice for a health profession. MCL 333.16221 (b)(i); MCL 333.16106(1).

In summary, of the six factual allegations outlined above, the Petitioner has established by a preponderance of the evidence that the Respondent violated Sections 16221(a) and 16221 (b)(i) of the Code concerning three of such alleged violations. MCL 333.16221 (a) and (b)(i).

The violation of Sections 16221(a) and 16221(b)(i) constitutes grounds for the Board of Medicine Disciplinary Subcommittee to proceed under Section 16226.

PROPOSED DECISION

I propose that the Board of Medicine's Disciplinary Subcommittee adopt the above Findings of Fact and Conclusions of Law, and issue a Final Order consistent with the above Conclusions of Law

Exceptions

If a party chooses to file Exceptions to this Proposal for Decision, the Exceptions must be filed within 21 days from the date of this Proposal for Decision. If an opposing party chooses to file a response to the exceptions, it must be filed within 14 days after Exceptions are filed. All Exceptions and Responses to Exceptions must be filed with the Michigan Administrative Hearing System, P.O. Box 30695, Lansing, Michigan 48909, and served on all parties to the proceeding.

Daniel Pulter Administrative Law Judge

CHAPTER 11

My Exceptions to the Proposal for Decision

◆ ◆ ◆

I FILED EXCEPTIONS ON TIME. I proved with indisputable evidence that all of the relevant facts were untrue. Among the evidence copies from three textbooks, even I shipped the textbooks to Mr. Hudson. Even if I did not file exceptions, nothing in the PFD would support any punishment. All of the three allegations that the ALJ ruled in are self-invalidated. The PFD is chapter 11, and my exceptions are this chapter. Anyone worldwide read them, would not find anything in the PFD justifies the devastating orders that damaged me, my family and thousands of patients in critical conditions and according to official documents; the Legislature and the Board of Medicine are aware that those kinds of patients, it was not easy for them to secure their medications.

THE STATE OF MICHIGAN

MICHIGAN ADMINISTRATIVE HEARING SYSTEM

Honorable Judge: Daniel Pulter Docket # 15-015505-BHCS

Board of Medicine, Bureau of Health Care Services

Vs.

Abdelbaset Abdelmagid Youssef Respondent

Dear Honorable Judge Pulter

Thank you for your honor giving me the last chance to defend me. Even it is the first chance to read Dr. Hopper testimony and have a chance to answer it. I cannot use my testimony alone for defense, for I am not credible enough to fight the credibility of the team of the petitioner and their expert witness. I will use, the Standard Text Books of Internal Medicine and Pain Management, and documents, the petitioner had produced into evidence.

A - Exceptions of Finding of Facts

Facts no. 7, 8, and 9: Mr. Regan has paranoid thinking about the patients, who, he never examined them. The 4 Pharmacies, he mentioned, one was cross street from my first office, one was in the same building of my 2nd office, one is close to my office, and the 4th is close to a group of patients. However, all of them stopped dispensing since Mr. Regan had visited them. He added pain to the patients' pain. However, every patient was able to secure his medicine from the mature pharmacists.

The fact no. 10 - Dr. Honet, the Pain management specialist, had issued 13,096 prescriptions in one year, while the respondent had issued 25,475 prescriptions in one year:

a - Dr. Honet is Anesthesia and pain management consultant. Traditionally the consultants should not keep the patients from giving only monthly Narcotics as a primary care physician, while the same patients go to their primary care physicians, to be given, the other medications,

b - Dr. Hornet, had issued more than 12000, prescriptions of DEA Schedule II, Narcotics, in one year, while the respondent issued only 85 prescriptions of DEA Schedule II, Narcotics in one year. The respondent issued only 7609 of DEA schedule III, just to keep the high potency schedule II Narcotics for the patient's future need because tolerance requires patients need an increase of narcotic equivalent by time.

Fact no.11- Morphine is DEA Schedule II, while Hydrocodone was DEA Schedule III. The Law allows giving script with five refills in Schedule III, but no refill for Schedule II. The highest dose of Hydrocodone is 10 mg, while the highest dose of Morphine is 200 mg; the 200 mg capsule of Morphine is equivalent to 20 tablets of Hydrocodone, {Exhibit no. B,}

Fact no. 17 - ten mg of Hydrocodone is equivalent to 750 mg of Morphine, {testimony of Dr. Hopper). This is False! 30 mg of Hydrocodone is equivalent to 10 mg injectable Morphine or 30 mg of oral Morphine. {Exhibit no. B; page 778, is a copy; from Mayo Clinic Internal Medicine Review} text book. He said that because Mr. Regan said: Dr. Honet prescribes; mostly Morphine and the respondent prescribe mostly Hydrocodone. However, the largest capsule of Morphine is 200 mg equivalent to 20 of the largest tablets of Hydrocodone. This is Clear Fraud to mislead the Judge!

Fact no. 18 - Dr. Hopper agreed, during the hearing that, Chronic Pain Syndrome causes Anxiety, Insomnia, and Depression. According to, {Exhibit no. C, textbook page 253}, Anxiety, and Pain should be treated together because each one exaggerates the other.

Facts no. 19 and 20 - A 1 mg dose of Alprazolam is the most potent dose. False! According to the {Exhibit no. D. is Harrison Textbook of Internal Medicine, the Worldwide Standard Text Book; page 76}. The starting dose of Alprazolam is 0.25 - 1 mg three times a day, so the starting daily dose is 0.75 - 3 mg, plus could be increased in later few days, but I gave Mr. B. S., just 1 mg a day, only for pain related Anxiety and Insomnia. However, there are tablets of Alprazolam up to 3 mg a tablet. The most potent daily dose is up to 10 mg.

Fact no. 21 - MRI is the best diagnostic test for Back Pain, {Exhibit no. C}, textbook page 1441, MRI of Mr. B. S. shows herniated discs and spinal stenosis. This is the best diagnostic for his pain and the related Anxiety and Insomnia.

Facts no. 22 and 23, according to (Exhibit no. C}; Text Book of pain management, page 1451 there is no treatment for chronic back pain with radiculopathy other than the Medications, with or without Surgery. The Functional Goal, in case of Mr. B. S. is to decrease his pain and its comorbidity and keep him functioning and working. No indication of Surgery at this time. Dr. Hopper agreed that no need for Physical therapy for working patient. Especially, who is working in construction; Physical therapy would not replace pain medicine.

Fact no. 24 – B.S got just 20 tablets of 5 mg of Diazepam. He took From a Nurse Practitioner. It is a muscle relaxant. He needed it and small amount. We use the MAPS, looking for the Doctor's Shoppers, who are visiting multiple MDs for selling medicine.

Fact no. 25 - According to B.S condition, I gave him the minimum, he needed. (Exhibit no. C) Text Book pages 145 and 2531. He has COPD from smoking. Smoking is one of the complications of Chronic Back Pain; he used to take, non-narcotic, cough medicine every visit. Just a few times he got Codeine cough medicine from my office and other MDs.

Fact no. 26 - Respondent has been running the MAPS, but no need for printing, if it was ok; so that there was no need for counseling. Respondent uses MAPS, but not like probation police officers to pick the criminals.

Facts no. 27, 28, 29, 30, 31 and 32: Dr. Hopper agreed that Chronic Pain causes, Depression, Anxiety, addiction, Social problems, such as Divorce, and many more. Mr. B. S.'s MAPS was clean; I am sure he was not addicted to Narcotics. I am not responsible for his work accident. I was not giving him high potency Narcotics such as Morphine, or other Schedule II. According to Testimony of his mother, we do not know anything, about what happened to him; even he refused to see a doctor. By any logic the respondent was blamed for things, nobody knows what it was. Just they saw one bottle of unknown medicine carry respondent's name, in the patient's home, is not enough for accusation! The mother stated that he has a history of Alcohol abuse and found him drunk and he had domestic trouble. His wife left his home, and he has five children with three women.

Fact # 33 - He needs to be followed by MD. I was giving him Motrin along with narcotics. But Motrin alone, he may take a high dose, much riskier than Narcotics.

Facts no. 34, 35, 36, 37, 38, 39, 40, 41, 42, 43, 44 and 45: Patient A. R., she had car accident 15 years ago, caused, MRI diagnosed anatomical damages all over the neck and lumbar discs. She had back surgery that failed, neck surgery was recommended, but she scared to do it. Back and neck surgery has 50/50 chance of success. She has other chronic medical problems, such as anxiety, Insomnia, asthma, allergic sinusitis, obesity, etc.

A - She is my patient for ten years, I am proud, she is still functioning and working on G.M. assembly line. She uses the same dose of narcotic; I am following her MAPS, her MAPS is 100% clean. She reports 10/10 pain without medicine, but medicine breaks the edge of pain and make the pain tolerable. This is her Functional Goal.

B - She takes a combination of controlled medications, all of these medications were indicated, and she is stable on these medications for 15 years. She does not need physical therapy as she is working. She does not need a referral to a pain clinic as they give spinal injections, all textbooks do not recommend it and high potency narcotics, which is too early for her age

C - According to the {Exhibit no. C; Text Book page 145}, there is no treatment for structural chronic back pain other than pain medicine, with or without surgery. It is a lifelong disease, like Diabetes and Hypertension. There is no other therapy replaces medications.

Fact no. 46 – A.R's record covers only six years, so four years is missing. I have been living in Inkster, and my first office is in Inkster. In August 2007, I bought a Bentley car at Auction. Inkster police thought, it is new, and I was rich. They complained to the DEA. The police and DEA raided my office on 10/04/2007. The main subject of the investigation was the car. The city police closed the office and sized everything except for the beds in my home. And the DEA took about 300 files, for review by physicians. The DEA cleared me. They did not find any wrong in any file. The city police had filed a forfeiture case. I win it from the first hearing, without an attorney. The Chief Judge of Wayne County Circuit Court ordered police to return all my stuff to my home. (Exhibit no. E. the Court Order When Mr. Regan asked about the file of A.R. I gave him what I had, and I gave him the Name and Phone No. of the DEA officer to get a copy for the missing four years, but he did not do.

Facts no. 47, 48, 49, 50, 51, 52, 53, 54, 55, and 56: Patient C. H. is my patient since 2009. She has, MR1 diagnosed, herniated discs and spinal stenosis all over her back, from the head to the sacrum. She had back pain with radiculopathy. She is not a candidate for surgery as there is no back transplantation. The functional goal is to break the edge of the pain and keep her functioning and exercising. She knows that her problem is lifelong chronic pain.

A - She is stable on her medications, I give her pain medicine and Xanax for pain related Anxiety and Insomnia, and I give her Adipex - P for obesity and as a stimulant to keep her active. I have been reviewing her MAPS; her MAPS is 100% clean. She did not need a referral to a pain clinic because pain clinic has nothing more to help her. She cannot has spinal injections for all of her spine, which are do nothing but more damage and she does not need high potency narcotics as Morphine or Oxycontin, as it is too early for her age.

B - As she has severe structural chronic back pain, no non-medication regime could replace her medicine. I give her combination of control medications, all of them were strongly indicated, and she was stable on them. Her functional goal has been achieved. However the combination of Xanax and Soma, I stopped to give since two years, because the State of Michigan dislikes it. Dr. Hopper agreed, during the hearing, that, there is no medicine that does not have a side effect, even drinking water.

C - Documentations, in her chart explain the needs of these medications, MRIs of all her back and neck, which is the gold standard for diagnosis of back pain, are in the file. She has back pain with radiculopathy, and pain-related Anxiety, Insomnia, and Obesity. I am writing as a Doctor to other Doctor. When I say COPD, any doctor knows what this means. I don't have to write lectures about COPD, or Obesity for teaching.

Facts no. 57 thru 67, Patient K. B., she is 60 years old lady. She has degenerative disc disease all over her spine, Osteoarthritis both hips and knees, chronic headache, lung doctor documented severe COPD, Anxiety, Depression, Hypertension, and obesity.

A - Functional Goal is to decrease her suffering as we could and keep her stable in good quality of life. She takes a combination of controlled medicine as strongly indicated. She was taking Lorazepam from her Psych. MD for three months in 2011. Gradually we decreased her needs for Benzo until she has been stable on Xanax 1 mg three times a day. Again, I am not probation police officer. Her MAPs is clean 100% for the last four years. I have been doing MAPS every visit for every patient. I discuss the risk of the medications, otherwise, how I stopped her from duplicating the 2 Benzo Medicines.

B - There is no option for surgery at this time or in the future. There is no non-medication regime replace her medications. Even physical therapy, even it may help but do not replace any of her medications.

Fact no. 68 - Physical Therapy improves the function, not pain management. I agree with Dr. Hopper. Physical Therapists accept Medicare patient only, even they refuse to do physical therapy for patients, who are not homebound. It is very expensive for cash patients.

Fact no. 69 - Medications Improve pain and Function, {Exhibit no. C, p145}.

Fact no. 70 - It is illegal to deprive the patient of treatment, as a punishment for refusal to take physical therapy, spinal injection, surgery, stop smoking, history of street drug abuse, or history of prison for a drug-related case or even addiction to controlled substances. The hospital should not be changed to be a criminal court.

Facts no. 71, 72, 73, and 74, Dr. Hopper testifies about other practices. I have nothing related to what he says.

Facts no. 75, 76, 77, and 80 - Combination of Hydrocodone and Alprazolam worsen the condition, is false testimony. This combination is required to treat both pain and Anxiety at the same time, as each one exaggerates the other, according to {Exhibit # C, Text Book page 253}.

Fact no. 81, false testimony! Dr. Hopper agreed during the hearing that chronic pain causes Anxiety. MRI is the gold standard for diagnosing back pain.

Fact no. 85 - Dr. Hopper had testified that Chronic Pain Syndrome could be treated by one or more controlled substances. This is true. Thanks for Dr. Hopper.

B - Exceptions for Conclusions of Law

Dear Honorable Judge Pulter:

Since your honor has given me a chance to defend myself regarding the Finding of Facts, and the Conclusions of Law are based on these facts, I hereby request if you may consider my defense and adjust the conclusions of Law accordingly. Concerning Mr. Regan and Dr. Hopper, I request if you may review their credibility at my statements on the finding of facts no. 10, 11, and 17, supported by Exhibits from standard textbooks.

A — Failure to consider the use of other treatment modalities or non-narcotic medications for treatment of pain

1. All of the four patients B.S., A.R., C.H., and K. B., I have been treating their pain by multiple non-narcotic medications

along with one narcotic, for example, B.S. was treated by NSAD, Acetaminophen, and Xanax. And patient K. B. I have been treating her for pain by NSAID, Fiorecet, Neurontin, Soma, Xanax, and Adipex-P; all of these are non-narcotic pain medications beside just one DEA schedule III narcotics.

2. In treating the patients, I am restricted by what I was learned, the standard textbooks, Federal and State regulations, and the condition of the patient in practice. I cannot send the patient for treatment, he does not need it, or he does not want it, or he cannot afford it. No one of these four patients are a candidate for physical therapy, spinal injection or surgery. These modalities require specific conditions. The Functional Goal has been achieved.
3. Petitioner is not aware of what non-medication modality. Petitioner has to tell me one of my patients was candidate for one of these modalities, and he was ready for it, and I deprived him of it

   If the petitioner asked me to fly in the air, I have the right to ask him how and why. I am not a research center. It is logical to ask me to do but exactly what I am required to do.
4. Attached here, (Exhibit no. C, copy from the textbook for pain management pages 144,145,252, and 253}, the petitioner may read it and compare it with what I have been doing. Or they may bring another textbook says different way.

B - Failure to consistently monitor for abuse and diversion by utilizing urine drug testing and checking patients prescription record with MAPS.

1. I was prescribing DEA schedule III; the Law gives the option to prescribe one month plus five refills. This means six month

supply. Mr. Regan, during the investigation, asked me to give refills as the Law permits. If I follow this recommendation, I have a chance to check the patient every six months. I check the MAPS for every patient, every visit, but I am not required that I have to print it and put it in the file, even if it is OK.

2. Urine test, if it is done on regular bases, it will lose its validity, because it is done to see if the patient takes medicine and if he uses cocaine. The patient is very easy to take a tablet just before the visit, and stop cocaine few days; the test result would be misleading. The valid urine test should be for suspected cases and surprise to the patient, as I was doing.
3. That patient K.B. took duplicate three times from her psychiatrist in 2011, and then she stopped to do that for the last four years, is indisputable evidence that I have been checking the patient's MAPS. At that time, the controlled substances were not posted in MAPS, until about 15 days after dispensing the medicine and MAPS reading was not easy like nowadays. The ethics and Law do not allow to through the patient who has chronic pain syndrome to the street for unknown fate, just because she duplicated without counseling, except for, if I was sure she is doctor shopper. I am not a probation officer.

C - Prescribing cm inappropriate combination of medications

Respondent had been treating patients with appropriate combinations. There is no FDA, or State regulations or official recommendations prohibit using this combination if it is indicated and used carefully. The risk is from the high dose but not from the multiple kinds with small doses. So far there are no official recommendations prohibit this combination if it is indicated. If this combination is inappropriate, the Bureau of Health Care should not hesitate to send a letter to prohibit it for releasing us from the responsibility of depriving the patients, who need it, before God and Law.

2. Anxiety related to Chronic Pain Syndrome, FDA approved the {Benzodiazepine} Xanax, as the first line of treatment. {Exhibit no. C, Textbook of Pain Management, Page 252}. The other non-controlled medications still under investigations for treating anxiety.
3. Carisoprodol is FDA approved muscle relaxant, recently became controlled. It gives better results than the other Muscle relaxants. The other muscle relaxants safer than Carisoprodol is not documented. Cheaper is not an issue, all of them are cheap.
4. The respondent does not start with high doses. That 10 mg Hydrocodone is equal to 750 mg Morphine was a hoax. 10 mg is equal to 10 mg oral or 3.3 mg injectable.

Mr. Regan in his testimony stated that the FDA sit 4 gram a day limit for Tylenol, but no high limit to the pure Narcotics. However, the starting dose of Hydrocodone for the naive narcotic patient is 10 mg 4 times a day. Mr. B. S., before he came to my office, he was on Hydrocodone 10 mg 3 times a day, but I started him on 10 mg 2 -3 times a day. After about 15 months, he was moved up to 10 mg 4 times a day, which was the same dose as the starting dose for narcotic naive patients. Regarding patients C. H. and K. B., they have been moved up to Hydrocodone

10 mg 4 times a day. The same dose of starting narcotic naive patients, even they have been on narcotics for many years. Regarding Patient A.R. she has been on narcotics for more than 15 years, just this year I moved her up to Oxycodone 30 mg 3 times a day.

I did not need to address conclusion of Law items D, E, and F as the ALJ did not rule in them and he dismissed them.

C - Conclusion

I, hereby request your honor may treat this case as a criminal case because if this decision executed, it will authorize the Board of medicine to revoke or damage my License. The decision is based only on a finding of facts, which almost all of them are just opinion of Dr. Hopper, which was not based on standard textbooks or any touchable evidence. Credibility alone is not solid evidence, as it is still the opinion of one person. The high academic level may do not replace the true field practice.

Accordingly, I request if you may adjust your decision to new decision, its bases include this appeal and file answer of the petitioner, if they have an answer.

Respectfully Submitted

Abdelbaset A Youssef

(313) 645 ****aastoria.medical@yahoo.com July 3, 2015

Board of Medicine Reviewed my Record in Four Minutes

On 7/3/2015, I filed my exceptions to the ALJ's PFD, as you may see it in the previous chapter, I considered myself unbelievable, so

I based all of the statements on undisputable evidence that included three textbooks, and even I shipped the textbooks to Mr. Hudson. I proved that all of the relevant facts were perjury under oath. Just for example finding fact # 15 the ALJ stated that I was giving his relative, patient B.S. 10 mg Hydrocodone and in the finding facts # 17, he stated that 10 mg Hydrocodone is equal to 750 mg Morphine. Any book from Tokyo to New York says 10 mg Hydrocodone equal to 3.3 mg injectable Morphine or 10 mg oral Morphine. The ALJ based his statements on testimony under oath of the expert witness Dr. Hopper. I do not blame the ALJ as he is not a physician. He just took the statement of a physician and put it on the PFD. This is just one example of the radicular finding of facts. The expert witness and the investigator testified under oath protected from suing for perjury by Quasi-judicial Immunity Doctrine. They do not try as they do not need even to hide their crime as their crimes are legally protected.

As per Law, I expected the Board of Medicine would review my exceptions, and they would clarify the cloud and call the Attorney General might prosecute these felonies.

R 792.10131 Proposals for decision. (1) When the final decision is made by a person who did not conduct the hearing or review the record, the decision, if adverse to a party other than the agency itself, shall not be made until a proposal for decision is served on the parties and an opportunity is given to each party adversely affected to file exceptions and present written arguments to the person who will make the final decision. On review of a proposal for decision, the final decision authority shall have all of the powers which it would have if it had presided at the hearing. (2) The proposal for decision shall be prepared by a person who conducted the hearing or who has read the complete record. A proposal for decision shall contain findings of fact and conclusions of law and analysis or rationale for conclusions. (3) A decision shall become a final decision in the absence of exceptions or review by an entity with final decision authority.

MCL333.16237(3) In reviewing the recommended findings of fact and conclusions of law of the hearings examiner and the record of the hearing, a disciplinary subcommittee may request the hearings examiner to take additional testimony or evidence on a specific issue or may revise the recommended findings of fact and conclusions of law as determined necessary by the disciplinary subcommittee, or both. A disciplinary subcommittee shall not conduct its own investigation or take its own additional testimony or evidence under this subsection.

(4) If a disciplinary subcommittee finds that a preponderance of the evidence supports the recommended findings of fact and conclusions of law of the hearings examiner indicating that grounds exist for disciplinary action, the disciplinary subcommittee shall impose an appropriate sanction under any combination of this article, article 7, or article 8. If the disciplinary subcommittee finds that a preponderance of the evidence does not support the findings of fact and conclusions of law of the hearings examiner indicating that grounds exist for disciplinary action, the disciplinary subcommittee shall dismiss the complaint. A disciplinary subcommittee shall report final action taken by it in writing to the appropriate board or task force.

According to the meeting time agenda; The Board of Medicine, Disciplinary Subcommittee, on 9/16/2015, in the bimonthly meeting, within four minutes, had reviewed my case record of hundreds of pages and voted for the next stated final order, which was destructive to thousands of people. As you see in the order they did not review my exceptions even they did not mention that I filed exceptions. Moreover, they did not state the presence of my exceptions, in violation of the Law. The Board of Medicine, Disciplinary Subcommittee claimed they adopted the Proposal of Decision without reviewing my exceptions to the PFD as described by Law. If they reviewed the

PFD without reviewing the Exceptions they might do because Mr. Hudson did not present the Exceptions to the Committee for review in retaliation for the personal conflict. Even if the Committee did not see my exceptions, they should not pass through the PFD itself. The false statements in the PFD are easily discoverable by any person who knows the basics of medicine. A medical assistant knows that the maximum daily dose of Xanax is not 1 mg or statement that I was giving the ALJ's relative 10 mg Hydrocodone and then 10 mg equal to 750 mg Morphine. Even if they did not review my exceptions or if I did not file exceptions, nothing in the PFD justify any punishment. Next is the final order suspended my license six months and later extended to be for good.

The STATE OF MICHIGAN
DEPARTMENT OF LICENSING AND REGULATORY AFFAIRS
BUREAU OF PROFESSIONAL LICENSING
BOARD OF MEDICINE
DISCIPLINARY SUBCOMMITTEE

In the Matter of
ABDELBASET A. YOUSSEF, MD File Number: 43-12-126661
License No: 43-01-081069 Docket Number: 15-015505-BHCS

FINAL ORDER

On September 18, 2014, an Administrative Complaint (Complaint) was executed that charged Abdelbaset A. Youssef, M.D, (Respondent) with violating sections 16221(a) and 16221 (b)(i) of the Public Health Code, 1978 PA 368, as amended; MCL 333.1101 et seq.

An administrative hearing was held in this matter before an administrative law judge who issued a Proposal for Decision on June 18, 2015, setting forth recommended Findings of Fact and Conclusions of Law.

The Disciplinary Subcommittee of the Michigan Board of Medicine (Disciplinary Subcommittee), having reviewed the administrative record, considered this matter at a regularly scheduled meeting held in Lansing, Michigan on September 16, 2015, and accepted the administrative law judge's Findings of Fact and Conclusions of Law in the Proposal for Decision. Therefore,

IT IS ORDERED that for violating sections 16221(a) and 16221 (b)(i) of the Public Health Code, supra. Respondent's license to practice medicine in the state of Michigan is SUSPENDED for a minimum of six months and one day, commencing on the effective date of this Order.

Section 7311(6) of the Public Health Code, supra, provides that a controlled substance license is automatically void if a licensee's license to practice is suspended or revoked under Article 15 of the Public Health Code. Pursuant to section 7311(6) of the Public Health Code, supra, Respondent's controlled substance license is automatically void, commencing on the effective date that Respondent's license to practice medicine in the state of Michigan is suspended.

IT IS FURTHER ORDERED that for the cited violations of the Public Health Code, Respondent is FINED $20,000.00 to be paid to the state of Michigan prior to applying for reinstatement of the license.

IT IS FURTHER ORDERED that the fine shall be mailed to the Department of Licensing and Regulatory Affairs, Enforcement Division, Sanction Monitoring, P.O, Box 30189, Lansing, Ml 48909. The fine shall be paid by check or money order made payable to the State of Michigan, and the check or money order shall display file number 43-12-126661.

IT IS FURTHER ORDERED that reinstatement of a license which has been suspended for more than six months is not automatic and, in the event Respondent applies for reinstatement of the license, application for reinstatement may not be made sooner than 90 days prior to the end of the suspension period and shall be in accordance with sections 16245 and 16247 of the Public Health Code, supra.

This Final Order is a public record required to be published and made available to the public pursuant to section 11 (1)(a) of the Michigan Freedom of Information Act, 1976 PA 442, as amended; MCL 15,241 (1)(a); and this action may be reported to the National Practitioner Data Bank and any other entity as required by state or federal law, in accordance with 42 USC 11101 et sea.

IT IS FURTHER ORDERED that in the event Respondent violates any provision of this Order, the Disciplinary Subcommittee may proceed to take disciplinary action pursuant to Michigan Admin Code, R 338.1632 and section 16221(h) of the Public Health Code, supra.

IT IS FURTHER ORDERED that this Order shall be effective 30 days from the date signed by the Disciplinary Subcommittee's Chairperson or authorized representative, as set forth below.

Dated: 10/30/2015

MICHIGAN BOARD OF MEDICINE

DISCIPLINARY SUBCOMMITTEE

CHAPTER 12

The Fox Law

◆ ◆ ◆

WHEN I WAS A CHILD, my grandmother told me a fiction story. The Fox found a Cockerel in a boat. The Fox asked the Cockerel why you sprayed dirt on my face. The Cockerel said: when? The Fox said: one year ago. The Cockerel said: but I am just six months old. The Fox said: so your father did.

On 10/30/2015, in the name of the Board of Medicine, the Assistant Attorney General as the attorney for the Board of Medicine entered an order for suspension of my medical License minimum six months and $20,000. My exceptions to the PFD were not reviewed in violation of the Law. All of the relevant facts of the PFD were perjury under oath. Even if I did not file Exceptions nothing in the PFD has legal value. If a person reads the PFD belongs to the medical field, he will discover that without my exceptions the ALJ's PFD still has not any legal value justify any punishment. The ALJ ruled in only three self-invalidated allegations. Here I am just presenting very short sentences from the PFD itself to show how the allegations are self-invalidated. Please read my exceptions in the previous chapters.

A - Failure to consider the use of other treatment modalities or non-narcotic medications for the treatment of pain!

Mr. Hudson through the complaint was writing about Tylenol as narcotic medicine while Tylenol is non-narcotic pain medication. Every patient in my office had at least one non-narcotic in addition to Tylenol. I have more than 6000 patients' charts. They did not assign any patient needed other treatment modality, and I deprived him of having it.

B - Failure to consistently monitor for abuse and diversion by utilizing urine drug testing and checking patients' prescription records with MAPS.

The ALJ himself stated in his PFD that he read a print from the MAPS for his relative, patient B.S. The MAPS is on the State website. Checking MAPS mean reading them on the website. No need for printing it in each visit and put huge amount print on the chart. All of the patients' MAPS are clean.

PFD finding fact # 13: *{13. Prior to treating patient B.S., the Respondent obtained a report regarding patient B.S. from MAPS. [Testimony of Dr. Hopper; Petitioner's Exhibit D at pp. 1-41 to 1-42.]*

C - Prescribing an inappropriate combination of medications.

They did not specify any patient, who I gave him a combination of medications or medicine the patient did not need it, or FDA does not approve it. Combination of Narcotic, Lorazepam, and Carisoprodol is FDA approved and it is indicated. Please read complete PFD and exceptions to it in the previous chapters. The ALJ statement that I was giving high doses, based on his finding fact #16 and 17.

Finding facts 16 and 17: He stated that I was giving his relative 10 mg Hydrocodone and 10 mg Hydrocodone is equal to 750 mg Morphine; this was perjury as 10 mg Hydrocodone is equal to 10 mg Morphine and ALJ's relative was taking 10 mg Hydrocodone from other physicians before he became my patient. Next is the ALJ's PFD finding facts # 16 and 17:

Fact # 16: *16. According to the MAPS report, patient B.S. had previously been treated with Hydrocodone-containing products. [Petitioner's Exhibit E.1]*

Fact # 17: *17. Ten mg of Hydrocodone is equivalent to 750 mg of Morphine. [Testimony of Dr. Hopper.]*

For these three self-invalidated allegations, my medical license was suspended for minimum 6 months, and then the suspension was extended to be for good; I was not able to get license in another state because my license in Michigan was suspended, I lost my practice that my family and I had built over 13 years, and thousands of patients mostly disable in critical conditions, stable in my office for about 10 years found themselves in helpless situation, injured and at risk of up to death.

CHAPTER 13

Judicial Review, the Big Hoax

◆ ◆ ◆

ORDER SUSPENSION THE MEDICAL LICENSE minimum six months and $20,000 fine. The order was subject to Judicial Review. I believed I had a great chance to win in the Michigan Court of Appeals. I filed a claim of appeal, and I filed a motion to stay enforcement of the order pending Appeal. The Court of Appeal denied the motion to stay for it should be decided in the Board of Medicine. Mr. Hudson, AAG was the attorney for the Board, so when we say the Board of Medicine means Mr. Hudson. I filed a motion to stay pending appeal to Mr. Hudson. He failed to respond to the motion by grant or deny. I had kept filing motions to stay five times in the Court of Appeals, due to MCR 7.209, every time I filed, the Court denied for Mr. Hudson did not decide the motion first.

MCL 24.304 Petition for review; filing, time; stay; record; scope.

A petition shall be filed in the court within 60 days after the date of mailing notice of the final decision or order of the agency, or if a rehearing before the agency is timely requested, within 60 days after delivery or mailing notice of the decision or order thereon. The filing of the petition does not stay enforcement of the agency action, but the agency may grant, or the court may order, a stay upon appropriate.

MCR 7.209 Bond; Stay of Proceedings: A motion for bond or a stay pending appeal may not be filed in the Court of Appeals unless such a motion was decided by the trial court.

If the enforcement of the order was not stayed the appeal was useless. It did not make sense that the person who issued the order was the only one who controls the staying its enforcement. I filed a motion to expedite the appeal. It was denied as well. The suspension was for six months, and the appeal took 18 months. What would I get from the appeal after 18 months? Judicial review was a big hoax. We should have the true appeal or no appeal.

Mr. Hudson acting as the Attorney for the Board of Medicine had failed to decide the motion for stay enforcement of the order, so that deprive the Court of Appeals jurisdiction on stay as MCR 7.209 do not allow the Court decide the stay unless it was decided first in the lower court. Mr. Hudson act was a violation of MCL24.304, so this act is intentional obstruction of justice. Obstruction of justice is a felony.

Next is the Court order denying staying five motions for pending appeal and order denying a motion for expedited appeal.

Court of Appeals, State of Michigan

ORDER

In re Abdelbaset Abdelmagid Youssef MD

Docket no. 330222. LC No. 15-015505

The Court orders that the motion for immediate consideration is GRANTED.

The Court orders that the motion for stay pending appeal is DENIED.

Copy entered and certified by Jerome W, Zimmer Jr., Chief Clerk, on date November 24, 2015

Court of Appeals, State of Michigan

ORDER

In re Abdelbaset Abdelmagid Youssef MD

Docket no. 330222. LC No. 15-015505

The Court orders that the motion for immediate consideration is GRANTED.

The Court orders that the motion for stay pending appeal is DENIED.

Copy entered and certified by Jerome W, Zimmer Jr., Chief Clerk, on date December 4, 2015

Court of Appeals, State of Michigan

ORDER

In re Abdelbaset Abdelmagid Youssef MD

Docket no. 330222. LC No. 15-015505

The Court orders that the motion for immediate consideration is GRANTED.

The Court orders that the motion for stay pending appeal is DENIED.

Copy entered and certified by Jerome W, Zimmer Jr., Chief Clerk, on date December 18, 2015

Court of Appeals, State of Michigan

ORDER

In re Abdelbaset Abdelmagid Youssef MD

Docket no. 330222. LC No. 15-015505

The Court orders that the motion for immediate consideration is GRANTED.

The Court orders that the motion for stay pending appeal is DENIED.

Copy entered and certified by Jerome W, Zimmer Jr., Chief Clerk, to date January 22, 2016

Court of Appeals, State of Michigan

ORDER

In re Abdelbaset Abdelmagid Youssef MD

Docket no. 330222. LC No. 15-015505

The Court orders that the motion for immediate consideration is GRANTED.

The Court further orders that the motion for reconsideration is DENIED.

Copy entered and certified by Jerome W, Zimmer Jr., Chief Clerk, on date February /22/2016

Court of Appeals, State of Michigan

ORDER

In re Abdelbaset Abdelmagid Youssef MD

Docket No. 330222 LC No. 15-015505

Michael F. Gadola, Judge, acting under MCR 7.211(E)(2), orders:

The motion for oral argument by appellant is GRANTED.

The motion to expedite appeal is DENIED.

I stopped to work in the office, but I left it open for few months to advise the patients and give them a copy of their charts to look for other providers. After I lost the hope of staying enforcement of the order, I closed my practice. My private practice was a business built over 13 years; it was started from one patient by closing, it had more than 6000 charts.

The legislature (MCL333.16204(2) The legislature finds that some patients in this state with pain are unable to obtain from their health care providers sufficient pain relief through the prescription of controlled substances, especially controlled substances included in schedule 2 under section 7214. And the guideline of controlled prescription says the same.

About 80% of my patients were officially considered disable and had Medicare insurance for their disability. Almost all of my patients were poor helpless and very sick. I used to examine some patients in the parking lot for they were not able to get out of the cars. Some patients were under treatment for addiction.

One time I had left the office for two-week vacation, the patients were worry of my absence, and they asked whether I had planned for them if something happened to me. As the Legislature stated, it was very difficult for the patients to secure pain doctor especially if they were coming from a sanctioned doctor. The stigma of sanction injures the doctor and the patients as well. Many patients were calling from the emergency room screaming and the ER doctors, who were calling me, were not able to help them and they asked if I could help the patients. Patients on narcotic pain medicine or addiction management could not wait, and they were at true risk of death. Due to stress, I was admitted twice to two hospitals for a heart problem.

Each patient in my office was a victim of this grave crime. The patients did not have a voice to cry on the reckless State officials. The patients, who are in pain or addiction medicine, feel guilty, for being sick as if they were responsible for their disease needs.

CHAPTER 14

I am not in North Korea

◆ ◆ ◆

AFTER THE DEVASTATING ORDERS THAT destroyed my assets and ruined my life and injured thousands of patients in critical conditions and put them at the risk of damage up to death, who would be blamed?

The problem started, on 9/18/2014, when Mr. Hudson Assistant Attorney General filed a complaint. He claimed that in 2009 patient C.H. was taking Tylenol 500 mg from another physician, but I gave her 750 mg when she became my patient. He believed Tylenol is controlled medicine, which is for sale in Gas Stations. I did not feel the smell of medicine at all in the complaint, so I stated in my response that the person who wrote the complaint either did not belong to the medical field or he was doing fraud. Mr. Hudson, who wrote the complaint, stated in the administrative hearing that because the subject of the complaint was outside his experience and considered me intentionally trying to defame him by addressing the defects in the complaint. My office's employees, who lost their job, blamed me. They said: I should not address the defects in the complaint that created the personal conflict.

I was investigated by Rosalie Tocco Bradley, MD. Ph.D., Pain Management Consultant and member of the Board of Medicine, stated that I was seeing very sick patients and I was doing well. The Board of

Medicine were absent had no authority on their business because the Legislature gives the authority to the assistant attorney general who was assigned to be an attorney for the Board. The authority was in the hand of Mr. Hudson, the attorney for the Board of Medicine; he was the one who makes the decision. Mr. Hudson asked me to pay $5000 fine. I refused to pay because he had to tell something wrong I had done for paying fine. He scheduled me for hearing before ALJ, who was a cousin of the complainant for her son. He got two other officials who told the ALJ grave lies about management of his nephew. They had been doing grave lies on the daylight without any shame. Just for example: here is one of the many grave lies; they told the ALJ that I was giving his nephew 10 Hydrocodone and 10 mg Hydrocodone equal to 750 mg Morphine while 10 mg is equal to 10 mg and Hydrocodone was DEA Schedule III, and Morphine was Schedule II. Since Schedule III was safer than Schedule II we are allowed to give the patient six month supply in refills but no refill for DEA schedule II.

Some of my patients blamed me for if I paid the $5000 fine, they would not be injured. One patient told my employees that if he had known, he would pay the fine from his money.

Even after all of perjury and frauds, the record did not justify any punishment, but they suspended my License for six months and $20,000. They used the Fox Law that a described in the previous chapter {The Fox Law}. The Fox Law means use anything to do any unjustified punishment.

In 1982, Egypt improved the Emergency Law, the new Law gives the officer the right to arrest any person without stating cause, but the victim has the right to challenge the arrest in the Court. The Court should issue a final decision within 45 days. People get happy because the maximum period of arrest without reason is 45 days. In real life, thousands of people had been arrested without cause for more than ten years. The officer would release the victim honoring the Court's order but he re-arrests the victim on the same page of the release. So the Law is just ink on paper. Everything is in the hand of the officer, who everybody should bow for him to stay safe. I believed that the Law should be blamed because it failed to protect people from tyrant officers.

Order for suspension of my License for minimum six months issued for personal conflict with Mr. Hudson, after a score of different kinds of felonies were done before the hearing, within the hearing, and after the hearing. The Law says the order is subject to judicial review in the Court of Appeals. I filed a claim of appeal but staying the order for pending appeal was in the authority of Mr. Hudson, who refused to stay enforcing the order for pending appeal. The Appeal would take 18 months, while the order itself was a suspension for six months. It did not make sense the Legislature gives the right for judicial review and keeps the key for stay enforcement of the order pending appeal in the hand of the same person that issued the order as retaliation for personal conflict, in the same time the appeal takes 18 months. Judicial review supposed to be invented to protect the victim from tyrant officers.

The hypocrisy in the Egyptian Emergency Law is similar to the hypocrisy of the American Judicial Review. The relief in both Laws is for export only, for the outside reader of the Law, who see it, fine relief, while it is a hoax. It is not for domestic use to give true relief. However, the Egyptians argue that their Law is acting in the status of emergency only, however status of emergency in Egypt is the norm. I do not remember Egypt has been ever in non-emergency status. The Egyptians further argue that their officers do not run the legal medical business which is outside their experience as they have full-time physicians run the medical side affairs of the medical-legal businesses. The legal officers' help is restricted to the legal side of the proceeding. The Americans argue that they cannot secure full-time physicians to run the medical side of the businesses as the physicians' salary in the USA is very high, so the Assistant Attorney General does everything for the practically absent Board of Medicine. The State can increase the License fee and secure full-time physician to investigate and write the complaint to the assistant attorney general.

According to my knowledge, the members of the Board of Medicine even they are very busy in their practices they travel to Lansing Michigan every two months to volunteer a day from their valuable time. I think they cannot do more than voting for the order prepared by the assistant attorney general. As per the agenda of the Board meeting, on 9/18/2015, they voted on 25 orders related to 25 physicians, mine was one of them within 94 minutes.

My attorney blamed me all the way. He stated I should not say that the writer of the complaint either he did not belong to the medical field or he was doing fraud. Mr. Hudson has all of the powers so I should not annoy him anyway. I did that because it did not come to my mind that the assistant attorney general was the one who wrote the complaint because the lawyer is far away from medicine. My attorney blamed me for not paying the $5000 fine and for filing an appeal. I felt, since I was in a Democratic and Constitutional State, I had the right to defend my rights legally. The attorney said that I could not take my rights by law in this country, I should do like other physicians, I would be submissive and just say I was sorry, I would not do it again and bow for them and be submissive in the hope they do the least damage.

I said to him, so we are in North Korea!

CHAPTER 15

False, fabricated documents

◆ ◆ ◆

AFTER I GAVE UP RELIEF from the appeal, I started preparing for the reinstatement. I sold my apartment in Florida and paid the fine and the attorney fee. The suspension was for minimum six months. I could apply 90 days before the end of the suspension period. The 90 days was for processing the application. I filed a complaint with Mr. Bill Schuette, Michigan Attorney General, may change Mr. Hudson the assistant attorney general, do an investigation or prosecute me for defamation. The Michigan Attorney General had never answered any of my complaints. By the end of the suspension period, Mr. Hudson presumed his retaliation as he filed a frivolous opposition to my application so that the application went through a hearing.

During the hearing, Jessica Taub AAG stated that: since I had filed an appeal, I was not eligible for reinstatement of the license. I stated that I filed an appeal because the order was based on perjury under oath. Jessica Taub filed false documents claiming that these documents were proof that I was in lack of good moral character. The documents were fabricated, and even if they were true, they did not establish lack of good moral character anyway. I had known that they would use these false documents to deny reinstatement by using the Fox Law that I described in a previous chapter {The Fox Law}.

Because my attorney's practice specialized in physician licenses, all his business comes through the assistant attorney generals. My attorney refused to file a motion to open record and remove false documents. If he filed this motion, he practically loses his business as physicians' license specialist attorney. I filed the motion away from my attorney. Next, you may read my motion:

The state of Michigan

MICHIGAN ADMINISTRATIVE HEARING SYSTEM

Abdelbaset Abdelmagid Youssef: Petitioner

V

Bureau of Professional Licensing: Respondents

Docket # 16-015746-BPL-HP Case # 43-10-141601

Case type: Reinstatement Agency:

Bureau of Professional Licensing,

Filling type: Board of Medicine

Administrative Law Judge: Honorable Peter L Plummer

Hearing Date was: July 5, 2016.

Petitioner's Motion to open record and put aside respondent's exhibits C. D. &E and testimony under oath.

Dear honorable Judge Plummer

I, Abdelbaset A Youssef, Petitioner in this case, hereby certify under penalty of perjury that the next statements, affidavits, and exhibits are true to my best knowledge.

1. Because of the kind of this motion, I hereby excuse my attorney from filing it.
2. The hearing was on 07/05/2016. The petitioner had presented clear, convincing evidence to prove that he is of good moral

character, has the reasonable skill to practice his profession and his work is in the public interest.

3. During the hearing, the Respondent had filed five exhibits. My attorney objected the last three exhibits (C, D, and E). The Respondent presented only one witness, who testified about these three exhibits, his testimony was objected as well.
4. I included in my affidavit that we filed along with the application for reinstatement on 05/05/2016 that: in 2013, I said to Mr. Regan that I have stopped giving a combination of Narcotic, Xanax, and Soma together in the same visit except for few patients, it is too risky to stop giving them this combination.
5. During the hearing, in response to the Respondent's question, I testified that the few means about 20 to 30 patients. This means, as of 11/29/2015. I still give this combination to about 30 patients.
6. The respondent presented exhibit # E stating that, during 2015, I gave this combination at least one time to 33 patients, and Presented exhibit # D stating that during 2014, 1 gave this combination, at least one time, to 334 patients and.
7. Presented exhibit # C stating that, during 2013, 1 gave this combination, at least one time, to 493 patients.
8. The State's only witness, under oath, testified that he copied this information from a reliable official source (MAPS).
9. The State used these exhibits and testimony as evidence to injure my credibility so that I look as if I am not of good moral character. Accordingly, I would not be eligible for reinstatement of my medical license.

10. When I went home, even I did not have access to the MAPS I was able to review charts of seven patients out of the 33 patients in exhibit # E. I found that I had never prescribed this combination to any one of these seven. So these exhibits are false. My Attorney feared to file a motion to remove these false documents from the hearing record. I filed the motion away from my Attorney. I presented the following:
11. I hereby present an affidavit supported by the patients" charts in Electronic Medical Record E.M.R., (this E.M.R. is Medicare approved, I cannot change anything of its contents)' proves that the Respondent's Exhibits and Testimony are inaccurate.

Analysis

A - Because a pharmacist told me that the State of Michigan Pharmacist disliked seeing this combination too often, 1 started to stop giving this combination. Since early 2013 to the end of 2014, the number of patients, who receive this combination decreased to less than 30 patients out of my office charts. My office contained more than 4000 charts for patients, who had chronic pain syndrome.

B - Exhibit # E: I testified under oath that I stopped giving this combination except for about 20 to 30 patients. Then, the respondent presented Exhibit # E, stating that during 2015, I was giving this combination to 33 patients. I reviewed the charts of the 33 patients; I found that I had not given this combination, in any visit during 2015, to 7 patients out of the 33. Attached is Exhibit # 1, and Exhibit # 2, (Medications lists for the seven patients), printed from E. M. R. This is indisputable evidence that I am a credible person.

E - This is indisputable evidence that Jessicas Taub's 3 Exhibits were not accurate and their witness did not tell all the truth. So I support my attorney in his decision to object admission of this evidence and testimony.

F – Respondents (Jessica Taub) could defend themselves by presenting the original hand signed prescriptions. I had been giving controlled prescriptions in signed forms only.

Requested Relief

I, pray the Honorable Judge may put aside these Respondent's three un-admitted and inaccurate exhibits and false testimony under oath, support my attorney in his decision to object admission of this evidence and testimony.

Respectfully submitted
Abdelbaset Youssef

After I filed the motion, Mr. Hudson and Jessica Taub, AAG failed to answer the motion. They practiced pressure on my attorney to make me withdraw the motion. Next, you may read the email from Jessica Taub, she asked him to withdraw the motion, and she gave the promise to resolve other cases from his firm. My attorney forwarded it to me to make me fear from their retaliation. I did not fear because there was nothing worse than what they had done, could be done.

Aaron J. Kemp akemp@chapmanlawgroup.com
To:astoria.medical@yahoo.com
Jul 12, 2016, at 11:53 AM
Dr. Youssef,

Please review the response from the AG below and confirm this is how you wish to proceed.

I would strongly recommend that the Motion is withdrawn, and you allow us to file this on your behalf, once it is properly redacted, as a petition for a post-hearing brief.

Let me know as soon as possible.

Thank you,

AARON J. KEMP, ESQ | Senior Attorney

"Providing superior legal services to all healthcare professionals at a reasonable and fair price!".

1441 West Long Lake Rd., Suite 310, Troy, MI 48098

Florida Offices:

Sarasota: 1834 Main Street, Sarasota, FL 34236

Miami: 5201 Blue Lagoon Drive, 8th Floor, Miami, FL 33126

Hollywood: 4000 Hollywood Blvd., Suite 555-S, Hollywood, FL 33021

Phone: (248) 644-6326 x2014

Fax: (248) 644-6326

Email: akemp@chapmanlawgroup.com

Web: www.chapmanlawgroup.com

From: Taub, Jessica (AG) [mailto:TaubJ@michigan.gov]

Sent: Tuesday, July 12, 2016, 11:45 AM

To: Aaron J. Kemp <akemp@chapmanlawgroup.com>

Subject: Youssef Motion

Hi Aaron,

I am not sure if you received a copy of the attached motion either from Dr. Youssef or our office, but this is what he submitted the other day. The last page of the PDF concerning

potential HIPPA violations was sent by Dr. Youssef separately. If Dr. Youssef's recent filing is to stand, I need to submit a response. If you could let me know by the end of the day how you will be handling his latest submission that would be appreciated.

Also, in the Daniels-Washington case, we are in the process of putting the file together for you, which will be mailed out to you either tomorrow or Thursday.

Thank you,

Jessica

From: Macias, Susan (AG)
Sent: Tuesday, July 12, 2016, 10:24 AM
To: Taub, Jessica (AG) TaubJ@michigan.gov
Subject: Youssef
Here is the Motion he filed.
Susan Macias, Legal Secretary
Attorney General
Licensing & Regulation Division
(517) 373-1146 maciass@michigan.gov

I responded to my attorney email that they would injure me anyway I wanted to keep the motion for Appeal later. Next, you may read my two emails to my attorney.

Abdelbaset Youssef astoria.medical@yahoo.com
To:akemp@chapmanlawgroup.com
Jul 11, 2016, at 11:30 PM

Dear Mr. Kemp

This case is not a clean legal proceeding. Mr. Hudson targets me as a person. The ALJ did not have the Authority of the final order, so the hearing is just decor. I filed the motion by myself to keep you away from this fight. Mr. Hudson worked hard to fabricate this evidence as he did before in the last hearing.

Please do not call the assistant attorney general. I want to keep my motion as I filed it.

I do not care if they complained about HIPA Violation.

I have the right to defend myself by the power I have. I need the motion to stay active as I filed it. It will help me later in case of the Appeal.

Thank You

Abdelbaset A Youssef

Abdelbaset Youssef astoria.medical@yahoo.com

To:akemp@chapmanlawgroup.com

Jul 12, 2016, at 12:37 PM

Dear Mr. Aaron

I am insisting keeping my motion active. They have to respond. I do not trust them.

Thank You

Abdelbaset Youssef

After Mr. Hudson and Jessica Taub had failed to respond to my motion, the Administrative Law Judge {ALJ} returned the motion in violation of Law to protect them. Next, you may read the ALJ's letter returning the motion for removal the false documents.

The state of Michigan

DEPARTMENT OF LICENSING AND REGULATORY AFFAIRS

MICHIGAN ADMINISTRATIVE HEARING SYSTEM

July 15, 2016

Abdelbaset Abdelmagid Youssef, M.D.

212 Cherry Lane Inkster, Michigan 48141

Abdelbaset Abdelmagid Youssef v Bureau of Professional Licensing

Docket No. 16-015746-BPL-HP

Dear Dr. Youssef:

The following documents that you filed with the Michigan Administrative Hearing System are being returned to you:

"Petitioner's Motion to open record and put aside Respondent's exhibits C, D & E and testimony under oath," received July 11, 2016; and

"Important Notice," received July 12, 2016, via facsimile.

These documents are being returned to you because they are not a part of the record in this matter and cannot be accepted after the hearing record was closed. The hearing record closed at the end of the hearing that was held on July 5, 2016.

Enclosures

Very truly yours,

Peter L. Plummer, Administrative Law Judge

Michigan Administrative Hearing System

CHAPTER 16

Negligence of the State Attorney General

◆ ◆ ◆

I FILED THE SECOND COMPLAINT to Bill Schuette, the State Attorney General. I requested if he may change the Assistant Attorney General for due to personal conflict, he was targeting me, do an investigation or prosecute me for defamation. Bill Schuette, the State Attorney General, had never responded to any of my complaints, and I had stayed for more than two years on the grill. Next is the second complaint that I filed in the office of the State Attorney General.

Honorable Bill Schuette

State of Michigan Attorney General

G, Mennen Williams Building 7th Floor

P. O. Box 30212, Lansing, MI 48909

COMPLAINT

I, Abdelbaset A Youssef, M.D., hereby raise to your honor this complaint: Because of a personal conflict with Andrew Hudson Assistant Attorney General, he and Jessica Taub Assistant Attorney general have conspired with the Administrative Law Judge Peter Plummer to commit a grave crime against me. They illegally delayed reinstatement of my license, and they are going to deny it. They use hunger, to defend the Appeal that I filed on 11/13/2015, against their order on 10/30/2015, suspending my license, instead of using the legal way.

Introduction:

1. The Board of Medicine had filed a complaint on 9/18/2014. After a compliance conference held on 11/4/2014, I refused an offer to pay $5000 in the settlement, and I requested a hearing.
2. After the Hearing, I filed Exceptions to the Proposal for Decision that ended by final decision suspended my License minimum six months and one day and $20,000 fine.
3. The final order was subject to Judicial Review; on 11/13/2015, I filed Appeal so that the Court of Appeals may review the Final Order.
4. On 2/11/2016, I submitted request to the Attorney General and the Bureau of Professional Licensing that Mr. Andrew Hudson, Assistant Attorney General, been conspiring with Mr. Ronald Regan R. Ph., and Hopper M.D., to subject me to severe cycles of torture as retaliation for personal issues, {Personal conflict during the hearing}, requesting to keep them away from my business to save me from deadly stress.
5. I applied for reinstatement of my license, just one day before the due date for reinstatement; Mr. Hudson, AAG, filed frivolous opposition that I am not honest, so the reinstatement went through a hearing.
6. On 7/5/2016, during the hearing, Jessica Taub, Assistant Attorney General, stated to the ALJ that I was not eligible

for reinstatement because I filed Appeal, I said that I filed the appeal because the hearing was infringed as the witnesses lied under oath.

7. She presented three documents and witness, who testified on these documents and stated that he took them from the MAPS which is a reliable source for proving I was not honest.
8. When I went home I discovered that these documents had been fabricated; I filed a motion with proof that they were not accurate but, after the AAG had failed to file an answer, the ALJ returned the motion for the record was closed, just to cover the AAG

About the Proposal for Decision

The ALJ filed frivolous PFD. He recommended that my application for reinstatement should be denied for I filed an appeal and by presenting intentionally wrong and misleading document.

1. I filed Appeal against the Board of Medicine final order, and the Appeal is still pending. During the hearing Jessica Taub, AAG said that I was not eligible for reinstatement because I filed Appeal. The ALJ said in the PFD finding facts 11 thru 14; Due to the short period of suspension, I still claim that I was tricked by the Authorities when I committed an act of incompetence ... etc. he recommended deny until I understand. This action is equal to; I am not hungry enough to give up my appeal. The order was suspension six months and one day, but now about one year. It is illegal to use filing appeal as a condition

for denying reinstatement; this is a criminal way to defend the Appeal. The Board of Medicine should defend the Appeal in the Court of Appeal in legal ways.

2. Because I am not immigrant from an English speaking country, I made a very little linguistic mistake in my affidavit. Instead of saying "I was stopping giving this combination gradually as stopping is risky," I said: "I have stopped this combination except for few patients, it is risky to stop it." During the hearing, the AAG asked me how much was the few, I said by guessing under oath that: from 20 to 30, she presented Exhibit # E, stating that they were 33. Later I discovered that even the Exhibits are incorrect as they were only 26 patients. For this grammatical mistake, the ALJ considered me Lack of Good Moral Character, so that I am not qualified to work as a physician anymore after 30 years of practice, while he made many intentional and unintentional mistakes.

The ALJ made the following mistakes in the PFD.

A - On page 11, he stated that I did not participate in a didactic or training program, while I did at Vanderbilt University School of Medicine, On February 3-5, 2016.

B - Finding fact # 9, Petitioner claimed in his affidavit P. Ex. 16, that "I have stopped prescribing of Narcotic, Soma, and Xanax since 2012. (It is not accurate!: I stated, "I stopped prescribing of Narcotic, Soma, and Xanax since 2012,1 told Mr. Regan R. Ph. (investigator) in 2013, that have stopped prescribing this combination, except for few patients, it is risky to stop it. {The right expression is stated up in item 2}.

C - In fact #10, ALJ stated that: Petitioner prescribed his potent and potentially deadly combination at least 493, in 2013, 334 in 2014, and 33 in 2015. Word deadly combination stated by Mr. Rivera, who is not a physician. This combination is FDA approved and it is the standard treatment for back pain due to spinal stenosis. Just around 2012 or 2013, after the FDA, classified Soma as controlled, voices appeared to avoid using Soma with Xanax and Narcotic at the same time. So Soma is better to be replaced by another muscle relaxant.

D - ALJ stated that: However the facts show that Petitioner was still writing a substantial number of his trinity prescriptions from 2013 thru 2014. Word still could not conform to 2014, because we are in late 2016. He should mention the non-admitted respondent's exhibit # E stated that the number of trinity prescriptions from 2014 thru 2015 was 33 then by late 2015, down to zero. So I am not still writing any combination contrary to the statement of ALJ; still writing a substantial number of his trinity.

E - On 07/08/2016, three days after the hearing I filed a motion to open the record and remove these three exhibits for I presented evidence that they are inaccurate. The AAG practiced pressure on my Attorney to make me withdraw the motion, so I retired him. By the due date, the AAG had failed to file a response, so the ALJ returned the motion for the record was closed; he did in violation of the law, just to cover the AAG.

F - On page 2 he stated that I applied for reinstatement on 3/3/2016, while my Attorney filed it on April 26, 2016.

G - On page 2, he stated my sons are M.D., while they are D.O. and page 12 denies qualification of them to be a witness. According to the opinions of the Court of Appeals, my sons are qualified to be expert witnesses and evaluators as they are specialized as I did, in Internal Medicine more than one year and have full unrestricted Licenses.

H - BFD page 11, the final order of the Board of Medicine was on April 7, 2014. Wrong, the final order was on October 30th, 2015. He intentionally made this mistake to cover his previous wrong statement.

I - On 2/11/2016, 1 filed request to the Attorney General and the Bureau of Professional Licensing about Mr. Andrew Hudson, Assistant Attorney General. He had been conspiring with Mr. Robert Regan R. Ph., and Hopper M.D., to subject me to severe cycles of torture as retaliation for personal issues, {Personal conflict during the hearing}. I was requesting to keep them away from my business to save me from deadly stress. Copy of this request attached here.

Conclusion

I am not seeking private justice I am requesting protection from clear criminal act from high power people. I filed Appeal to defend myself from an order I believe it is not fair and it is subject to Judicial Review, it takes 18 months to get a result. Now because I filed Appeal I have been punished, and I have to file another Appeal for a new order of denial my reinstatement it will take another 18 months, then further retaliation for the second Appeal. Because this order I am not able to seek License in another State.

I am calling from under water. I pray your honor may protect me.

Respectfully Submitted
Abdelbaset A Youssef. On 9/28/2016.

CHAPTER 17

Quasi-judicial Immunity, the illegal extension

◆ ◆ ◆

JUDICIAL IMMUNITY IS JUDGE'S COMPLETE protection from personal liability for exercising judicial functions.

Judicial immunity protects judges from liability for monetary damages in civil court, for acts they perform pursuant to their judicial function. A judge would have immunity from civil damages if she had jurisdiction over the subject matter in issue. This doctrine means that a judge has immunity for acts relating to cases before the court, but not for acts relating to cases beyond the court's reach. For example, a criminal court judge would not have immunity if he or she tried to influence proceeding in a juvenile court. Some states codify the judicial immunity doctrine in statues. Most legislatures including Congress, let court decision govern the issue. Judicial immunity is a common law concept, derived from judicial decisions. It originated in the courts of medieval Europe to discourage persons from attaching a court decision by using the judges instead taking their complaints to appellate courts.

A quasi-judicial body is an entity such as an arbitrator or tribunal board, generally of a public administrative agency, which has powers and procedures resembling those of a court of law or judge, and which is obliged to objectively determine facts and draw conclusions from them to provide the basis of official action. Such actions can remedy a situation or impose legal penalties and may affect the constitutional rights, duties or privileges of specific parties.

Such bodies usually have powers of adjudication in such matters as:

Breach of discipline, such as physician disciplinary proceeding,

Conduct rules, or trust in the matters of money or otherwise

Their powers are usually limited to a particular area of expertise and authority, such as land use and zoning, financial markets, employment law, public standards, or a specific set of regulation.

There are some key differences between judicial and quasi-judicial bodies, in that:

Judicial decisions are bound by precedent in common law. Whereas quasi-judicial decisions usually are not so bound;

In the absence of precedent in common law, judicial decisions may create new law, whereas quasi-judicial decisions must be based on conclusions of existing law;

Quasi-judicial bodies need not follow strict judicial rules of evidence and procedure;

Quasi-judicial bodies must hold formal hearings only if mandated to do so under their governing laws or regulations

Quasi-judicial bodies, unlike courts, may be a party in a matter and issue a decision thereon at the same time;

In general, decisions of a quasi-judicial body require findings of facts to reach conclusions of law that justify the decision. They usually depend on a pre-determined set of guidelines or criteria to assess the nature and gravity of the permission or relief sought, or of the offense committed. Decisions of a quasi-judicial body are often legally enforceable under the laws of jurisdiction; they can be challenged in a court of law which is the final decisive authority.

Quasi-judicial immunity extends judicial immunity to persons who are integral parts of the judicial process, such as prosecutors, court-appointed mediators and others lawfully acting or assisting in a judicial role. Quasi-judicial immunity has increasingly been extended to state and local officials, such as a director of a County Human Relations Commission:

The federal court stated that: Assuming that plaintiff has stated a claim for damages against the defendant Commission members and defendants Byrd, Davis, and Stevens under section 1981, section 1985, or the Fourteenth Amendment, such claims are barred by the doctrine of quasi-judicial immunity. [Commission] Director Byrd was acting in a manner functionally comparable to a judge. Specifically, under the Ordinance, the Commission delegated authority to Director Byrd to dismiss a charge. See Ordinance. When he dismissed plaintiffs charge, he did so "on behalf of the Commission." Adequate procedural safeguards exist under the Ordinance in the form of a judicial de novo review of Commission decisions. Thus, Director Byrd is entitled to absolute quasi-judicial immunity. Likewise, Investigator Davis and Investigator Stevens were obligated to investigate plaintiff's allegations and make a recommendation to the Commission regarding plaintiff's charge. See Ordinance. This "evidentiary review was necessary to determine whether to pursue charges, and a prosecutor is held to be absolutely immune from liability for performing such duties." As such, Investigators Davis and Stevens also are entitled to absolute quasi-judicial immunity. See id. (Physician conducting a peer review at behest of a physician's board entitled to absolute quasi-judicial immunity); Fares v. United States INS, 29 F. Supp. 2d 259, 262-63 (W.D.N.C. 1998). Alternatively, even if Investigators Davis and Stevens are merely entitled to qualified immunity, the court grants the defendants' motion for summary judgment.

I had two judicial proceedings one in the Federal Court before Honorable Judge Victoria Roberts and one in the Michigan Court of Claims before Honorable Judge Michael Talbot and one quasi-judicial proceeding in Michigan Board of Medicine, Disciplinary Subcommittee before Mr. Andrew Hudson, Assistant Attorney General who was an attorney for the Board of Medicine.

I am comparing the Judicial and Quasi-judicial proceeding to see if it is appropriate to extend the absolute Judicial Immunity to the Quasi-judicial people.

For the next reasons, it was not appropriate to extend the Judicial Immunity to the Assistant Attorney generals or the State officials and employees. Some state officials use this doctrine as a back window for committing crimes under the protection of the law in violation of the Constitutions, Democracy, and human rights values.

1 – The judge in my Federal Court proceeding was Honorable Victoria Robert, like any other federal Judge she was elected by the office of President of the United States and the U.S Senate approved the election for her superior Curriculum Vitae. While the Judge on the Board of Medicine was Mr. Andrew Hudson, Assistant Attorney General, he filed the complaint against me about two years after his graduation in a law school. On the official paper, they were claiming that the proceeding was done by the Board of Medicine, which is in real life was not true. The members of the Board are very busy physicians; every two months travel to the state capital as guests coming from all over the state for few hours meeting, just for coffee and voting for orders. On 9/16/2015, they reviewed 25 records and voted for 25 orders related to 25 physicians including my file, within 94 minutes. Their election to be members of the Board of Medicine was an honor for their excellence in practicing medicine, but their experiences in

law were not known. The membership is nothing more than such an honorary membership in a social club. Mr. Hudson was their Attorney, but he had been doing everything. The Administrative Complaint that was filed by Mr. Hudson did not have a smell of medicine as an example, the writer, through the complaint, was talking about Tylenol as the controlled medicine and nothing else had legal value as a complaint in the management of chronic pain syndrome. This was proof that it was not seen by any member of the Board of Medicine or even anyone belongs to the medical field such as a nurse had reviewed it. So the real judge in the Board of Medicine proceeding was Mr. Hudson, Assistant Attorney General. The members of the Board of Medicine have nothing to do at any stage of the proceeding. *So the Federal Judge in the court proceeding is in comparison with Mr. Hudson as the judge for the quasi-judicial proceeding.*

2 – Honorable Federal Judge Robert did not come to me but I went to her in the court when I filed my complaint, and I was able to ask her honor to recuse herself if I needed as I did in my proceeding in the Michigan Court of Claims. In case of the Board of Medicine proceeding, their judge was Mr. Hudson, who filed the complaint, so he came to me, and because of a personal conflict he targeted me by severe accelerated retaliations that ruined my life and injured thousands of patients, and I could not escape from his hand. I could not make him recuse himself. I filed complaint twice to Mr. Bill Schuette; Michigan Attorney General and I told The State Attorney General that, due to personal conflict, Mr. Hudson had been conspiring with others and doing felonies against me and he was ruining my life and destroying my assets and injured thousands of patients in critical conditions. I requested he may change him, do an investigation, or prosecute me

for defamation. The Attorney General has never answered any of my complaints. I sent the same complaints to the Board of Medicine, they did not, and they could not do anything as they had no authority on Mr. Hudson or in the matter at all. The Board of Medicine, even they are presumed to be the Judge they have not had any authority in the proceeding. The Michigan Law makes an assistant attorney general attorney for the Board of Medicine. In case of any general public case, the attorney takes control of his client business. Even the client in the general public cases can change their attorney, but here the Board of Medicine could not change the assistant attorney or even interfere in his work as he is appointed to be their attorney by the legislature:

MCL333.16237(2) The department of attorney general may assign an independent special assistant attorney general who is under contract to the department of attorney general and is not a member of the state classified civil service to advise the disciplinary subcommittees on matters of law and provide other legal assistance as necessary.

This means, in the legal standpoint, the Board of Medicine is the assistant attorney general.

I sent a copy of these complaints to Mr. Hudson in the hope he might recuse himself instead he accelerated the retaliation to be the suspension of the medical license for unlimited years instead of the suspension for six months. The Michigan Attorney General had never answered any of my complaints. *Immunity of the Board of Medicine means immunity of Mr. Hudson. The name of the Board of Medicine just is borrowed as a tent for hiding from the Law, and then Mr. Hudson runs the professional business, which he did not know its basics.*

3 – Honorable Federal Judge Robert was not a party in the case, but Mr. Hudson who was the judge in the Board of Medicine proceeding

was a party as the argument with the Board was ended in the early beginning when I was investigated by Rosalie Tocco Bradley, MD. Ph.D. Pain Consultant and Member of the Board of Medicine, she told me that I was seeing very sick people and doing well, so the Board of Medicine practically signed off. Mr. Hudson, out of the control of the Board, had kept the case for retaliation for what he believed that I was intentionally trying to defame him when I addressed the defects in the complaint. First, he asked me to pay $5000 fine, after I refused to pay, he changed the punishment to be six months suspension of the medical license and $20,000. After I filed Appeal, the suspension was extended to be for countless years as they claimed that since I filed the appeal, I still did not admit my mistake, so I was not eligible for reinstatement of the License.

4 – Honorable Federal Judge Robert could not choose witness of her choice or conspire with them as she had not had control on them. If the witness committed perjury, only the prosecutor would prosecute them. In the Board of Medicine proceeding, Mr. Hudson selected the witnesses, who committed perjury under oath about management of patient B.S. Patient B.S. is the nephew of the ALJ conducting the hearing. Mr. Hudson was the only one who could prosecute the witnesses for perjury, but instead, he made haven to them as they were doing the perjury upon his order and he selected the Administrative Law Judge who is the cousin of the complainant. Mr. Hudson, the witnesses, and the ALJ were state officials work in the same agency.

5 – Honorable Federal Judge Robert controls the behavior of the witness and the prosecutor and hears both parties of the proceeding and issue the final order. In the Board of medicine, the ALJ has not had the authority to issue the final order, he works as a magistrate judge

or referee, just does the hearing and makes the preliminary proposal of decision {PFD}, and the Board of Medicine does the final PFD and the final order. While this job claimed to be done by the Board of Medicine but in real life, Mr. Hudson does this job as he is the attorney for the Board of Medicine, appointed by law. The Board of Medicine is absent, and Mr. Hudson does all the business, professional and legal. He was the writer of the complaint from his medical knowledge, the prosecutor, the witness and the judge who writes the final order. All were done at the same time, in the same case by one person, absolutely immune and he is above the law.

In 2010, people filed complaints about Farid Fata, MD. He was a Catholic Oncologist was doing fraud, he was giving Chemotherapy to healthy people and who had terminal hopeless malignant diseases for money. The Board of Medicine dismissed the complaints, and after three years the Federal Government prosecuted him, and he was sentenced to spend 45 years in the federal prison for the same claims that the Board of Medicine had dismissed. Because the Board was absent the complaints against Dr. Fata were dismissed. Because the Board of Medicine was absent, my license was suspended for years. My practice that my family and I had built over 13 years was destroyed and thousands of patients under treatment for chronic pain and addiction stable for about ten years, most of them officially disable in medically underserved cities found themselves in the street, medically homeless.

6 - In the court preceding the Judge acts as only Judge. In the Board of Medicine proceeding, Mr. Hudson, who has graduated two years ago in a law school was the judge. H filed the complaint in controlled prescriptions using his medical knowledge, in violation of MCL333.16228. He selected the ALJ who was the cousin of the complainant, picked the witnesses and made haven to commit perjury

under oath. He prosecuted the case in a hearing where he committed false statement and brought the wrong report. He reviewed my exceptions to the PFD and issued the final order and presented it at the Board bi-monthly meeting for voting.

7- The Honorable Federal Judge Robert's decision, I was able to appeal it to the 6th Circuit Court of Appeals. Mr. Hudson's order of suspension the License 6 months was subject to judicial review in the Court of Appeals. After I filed a claim of appeal, Mr. Hudson refused to stay enforcement of the order; even he refused to decide it so that the Court of Appeals could not stay it. The Court of Appeals had not had jurisdiction on the stay if Mr. Hudson did not decide it. The appeal took 18 months while the order itself was for six months, so the appeal became useless. After six months I filed for reinstatement of the License. Mr. Hudson and Jessica Taub, AAG denied reinstatement, and on an official document, they claimed since I filed appeal I did not admit my mistake, so I was not eligible for reinstatement. The suspension was extended from six months to be for years, and the Court of Appeals had not had jurisdiction on the extension of the suspension. So the Judicial Review was a big hoax. If I did not file the appeal, the suspension would be six months but because I filed the appeal the suspension was extended for years.

For the previous reasons and other reasons, extending the judicial immunity to state officials and employees creates tyrants committing felonies under full protection of the law. The quasi-judicial immunity became a back window for committing crimes under the daylight. The regular felons are trying to hide their crimes, but in my case, the legally protected felons did not have interest in hiding their crimes. This immunity is a grave wound in the protection of the constitutional and democratic values.

CHAPTER 18

Serven Vs. Board of Chiropractic

◆ ◆ ◆

ABSOLUTE QUASI-JUDICIAL IMMUNITY OF the state officials created sect of noble people above the Constitutions and Laws a state official called it higher level. They are armed by the office of the State Attorney General. They make over protected community similar to the Church in the middle ages in Europe. They line up with each other to defend their interests and corruptions illegally. If anyone of the general public injured or just touched anyone from the State community or related to any one of them, his life will be ruined. I was not the first one or the last to be destroyed and thousands of his patients injured and suffered. Hundreds of physicians have been injured by non-sense complaints and felonies of obstruction of justice under the haven of the absolute quasi-judicial immunity.

I present two similar cases where the state officials lined up for touching interest of one of them. My case, a lady complained that I was giving her son narcotic while he was able to control his pain by Motrin. FDA does not approve Motrin for treating chronic pain syndrome resulted from construction work accident and MRI documented herniated disc and spinal stenosis and radiculopathy. Because the lady is a cousin of Administrative Law Judge works in Licensing and Regulatory Affairs, {LARA}, Mr. Hudson, Assistant Attorney General who works at LARA as well, filed a complaint against me. He stated that in 2009, I gave patient CH combined medicine contains Tylenol 750 mg while she was taking one contains Tylenol 500 mg from another doctor before she came to my office. Mr. Hudson selected the same Administrative Law Judge {ALJ} cousin of the complainant to conduct the hearing; other officials had committed grave perjury under oath about my management of the ALJ's nephew. They can use anything to do anything.

Another case similar to my case; Dr. Bruce Serven, Chiropractic examined a patient his name A. E. The patient was referred to him by State Farm Insurance Company to see if he needed Chiropractic work. Dr. Serven discovered that he did not need this kind of treatment. The Insurance Company stopped to pay for Health Quest of Burton Chiropractic, PC.

Dr. Solomon Cogan was the co-owner of Health Quest, and he was the Chairman of Michigan Board of Chiropractic. Dr. Serven alleged that Dr. Cogan threatened him, "Obviously I need to see you on a higher level." The Assistant Attorney General filed a complaint against Dr. Serven, and through quasi-judicial executive proceeding Dr. Serven was punished for one-year probation, later the Court of Appeals found it illegal punishment and reversed it. Dr. Serven filed a complaint about damage in the Circuit Court, which denied Dr. Cogan and the other State Officials' motion for summary disposition. The Court of Appeals dismissed the case in favor of Dr. Cogan, and the other State Officials for they were shielded by absolute quasi-judicial Immunity against any wrong even it was done intentionally.

THE STATE OF MICHIGAN

COURT OF APPEALS

FOR PUBLICATION April 6, 2017, Docket No. 330983

BRUCE D. SERVEN,

Plaintiff: Appellee,

Vs.

HEALTH QUEST CHIROPRACTIC, PC, SILVIO COZZETTO, CHRISTOPHER DEAN, RANDY WILCOX, MICHIGAN BUREAU OF HEALTH PROFESSIONS-BOARD OF CHIROPRACTIC, and QUEST HEALTH SYSTEMS VI, PLLC, HEALTH QUEST OF BURTON, and SOLOMON COGAN, THOMAS KLAPP, and RONALD WILCOX,

Defendants: Appellants.

Before: O'**Connell**, P.J., and **Gleicher** and **Boonstra,** JJ.

PER CURIAM.

Bruce D. Serven is a chiropractor who was disciplined by the Disciplinary Subcommittee of the Michigan Bureau of Health Professions-Board of Chiropractic. This Court reversed the subcommittee, holding that its order lacked legal and factual merit. Serven then filed suit, alleging that the disciplinary subcommittee members acted with self-interest and improperly penalized him. As to the part of Serven's claims, the circuit court denied the disciplinary subcommittee members' motion for summary disposition based on quasi-judicial immunity and qualified immunity as well as failure to state a claim upon which relief could be granted. Because the disciplinary subcommittee members were entitled to absolute immunity as quasi-judicial actors, we reverse and remand for further proceedings consistent with this opinion.

Background

This case arises out of State Farm Insurance Company's retention of Serven, a licensed chiropractor, to perform an independent chiropractic examination (ICE) on AE. AE had been involved in a motor vehicle accident in May 2004 and two years later sought chiropractic treatment from Health Quest of Burton. Health Quest treated AE approximately three times weekly. At the time, Health Quest was owned, in part, by Solomon Cogan and Silvio Cozzetto. Cogan was also the chairman of the Michigan Bureau of Health Professions-Board of Chiropractic. Defendants Thomas Klapp and Ronald Wilcox were members of the board's disciplinary subcommittee.

Serven conducted a physical examination of AE and elicited his medical history. Serven concluded that AE was "not currently suffering from any musculoskeletal condition of spinal origin of causal relationship to the [subject] auto accident." In fact, Serven opined that AE's condition was "normal," negating the need for any further chiropractic services. Serven further advised State Farm that Health Quest's services provided to date were not "medically necessary for the injuries sustained in this accident." Based in part on this advice, State Farm denied payment for additional treatment to AE. Health Quest filed suit against State Farm, seeking reimbursement for the services Health Quest had provided to AE; Serven and Cogan testified against each other during the trial. State Farm prevailed. Serven alleges that Cogan threatened him, "Obviously I need to see you on a higher level."

Shortly after that, Cogan's business partner, Cozzetto, filed a complaint against Serven with the board. Cozzetto noted that he was sent by his own insurer to Serven for ICE following a 2000 car accident. Cozzetto alleged that Serven conducted chiropractic and orthopedic tests improperly, leading to an inaccurate report and termination of his insurance benefits. In relation to the current matter, Cozzetto indicated that his associate, Dennis Borja, had examined and treated AE. Cozzetto accused Serven of improperly rendering an opinion without reviewing Health Quest's records and acting outside the scope of his chiropractic license by considering records from medical care providers. The Attorney General subsequently filed an administrative complaint against Serven, alleging that his behavior constituted negligence, incompetence, and lack of good moral character under MCL 333.16221 of the Public Health Code, MCL 333.1101 *et seq.* The lack of good moral character allegation was based on Serven's alleged comment during the board's investigation that Health Quest "had a track record of performing the unnecessary treatment." The case was referred to an administrative law judge (ALJ) who determined that Serven was not negligent, incompetent or lacking in good moral character and the ALJ issued a proposal for a decision to this effect.

The disciplinary subcommittee of the board did not adopt the ALJ's proposal. At a March 15, 2012, meeting at which Cogan was present, the subcommittee instead found that Serven was negligent because he had not reviewed Health Quest's chiropractic records before issuing his opinion regarding the ICE. In addition, the subcommittee determined that it was "quite likely" that Serven commented that Health Quest "had a track record of performing unnecessary treatment," representing a lack of good moral character. The board placed Serven on probation for one year. Serven appealed the disciplinary subcommittee's decision in this Court.

Ultimately, as the board's disciplinary subcommittee was cloaked with absolute quasi-judicial immunity; the circuit court should have dismissed Serven's claims against these defendants. Given this resolution, we need not consider the remainder of defendants' appellate challenges.

We reverse and remand for further proceedings consistent with this opinion. We do not retain jurisdiction.

CHAPTER 19

List of the Legal Felonies

◆ ◆ ◆

THE TERM FELONY, IN SOME common law countries, means a serious crime. The word originates from English common law where felonies were originally crimes that involved confiscation of a convicted person's land and goods. Other crimes were called misdemeanors.

The felonies are classified by violent or nonviolent, according to its seriousness, and by subject matter.

Crimes against justice, such as malfeasance in office, miscarriage of justice, obstruction of justice, filing false documents, fraud, perverting the course of justice and perjury are examples of felonies about legal proceedings.

Discrimination in hiring for job or housing is a crime, but it is legal if it was done against felon. The Federal Court and the State Court decided that due to absolute quasi-judicial immunity, we cannot sue state officials for felonies against justice such as perjury and obstruction of justice if they did these acts about a quasi-judicial proceeding such as physician disciplinary proceeding. Honorable Michael Talbot, Michigan Court of Claims asserted that ("Falsity or malice on the part of the witness does not abrogate the privilege"). My understanding, since law protects these crimes, they can be called legal felonies.

A final order entered on 10/30/2015, suspension my medical license minimum six months and one day and $20,000 fine. My son filed a complaint with Michigan Governor stated that they suspended my father's license without cause. The Director of Bureau of Professional Licensing stated that I refused to pay $5000 fine in settlement and still I had a chance for appeal. The only answer they ever had is that I refused the settlement and the suspension were done after hearing, and I had a chance of appeal.

The Federal Courts and State Court decided that I could not sue the state officials for damages resulted from crimes once they did them within or about executive proceeding such as physician disciplinary proceeding. The Court could not enjoin their continuous violations because they were shielded by absolute quasi-judicial immunity equal to judicial immunity of Judges in the courts.

The felonies were done about the executive proceeding are protected by law, they are legal felonies.

The following felonies were done about Board of Medicine, Disciplinary Subcommittee proceeding and I could not sue the state officials for these felonies in federal or state court because absolute quasi-judicial immunity shields the state officials.

LEGAL FELONY # 1 – Mr. Andrew Hudson, AAG wrote the complaint about controlled medicine based only on his knowledge while he did not know the basics of medicine. The MCL 333.16228 requires ten physician panel should review this kind of complaints. Even he was authorized to write it he should not write it by this way. This act caused personal conflict that became the seed for all of the devastating damages to me, my family and thousands of critically ill patients.

My medical license authorized me to do any surgery, but if I did any without training, even if it were successful the act would be a felony. A person, who drove a car while he does not know how to drive and injures people, committed a major felony. Mr. Hudson act was gross negligence or a felony, but absolute quasi-judicial immunity protected him, so law protects this felony; **{Legal Felony}.**

LEGAL FELONY # 2 – Mr. Hudson intentionally selected the Administrative Law Judge, who was a cousin of the complainant and witness in violation of the constitution that requires the state official prosecute me before a fair and unbiased tribunal, this act is obstruction of justice; **{Legal Felony}.**

LEGAL FELONY # 3 – Mr. Hudson gave a false statement to the ALJ about the discovery of documents and presented report contains incorrect information, and information about three unknown patients which were fraud and obstruction of justice; **{Legal Felony}.**

LEGAL FELONY # 4 – Mr. Hudson conspired with Mr. Robert Regan and Dr. Hopper to commit grave perjury under oath about my management of the ALJ's nephew. He made a haven for them as he is the only one who could prosecute them. I gave him strong evidence including I shipped to him three textbooks proof that they did perjury, but he did not prosecute them or remove their testimonies from the record; **{Legal Felony}**

LEGAL FELONY # 5 – Mr. Robert Regan, investigator, committed, under sunlight grave perjury under oath about my management of the ALJ's nephew and other issues; **{Legal Felony}**

LEGAL FELONY # 6 – Dr. John Hopper committed grave perjury under oath about my management of the ALJ's nephew and other patients; **{Legal Felony}.**

LEGAL FELONY # 7 - Dennis Szymanski, M.D., member of the Board of Medicine presented the order for suspension of my license to the committee for voting without reviewing my exception to the proposal for decision in violation of Michigan Legislature, MCL 333.16237 and R.792.10131. This act was obstruction of justice caused devastating injury and damage to thousands of people; **{Legal Felony}**

LEGAL FELONY # 8 – The Members of Disciplinary Subcommittee adopted the ALJ's Proposal for Decision {PFD} conclusions of law and voted for devastating order while there was nothing in the PFD justifies any punishment. All of what stated in the conclusions were that the ALJ found me negligent because the Expert Witness told him that I was giving his nephew 10 mg Hydrocodone and 10 mg Hydrocodone is equal to 750 mg Morphine. Any medical assistant or nurse knows the 10 mg is equivalent to 10 mg, so the ALJ stated that I was giving patients high dose. The ALJ stated that I was giving an inappropriate combination of medications because the witness told him this, which was false. All of the combinations were FDA approved for the kind of disease. The ALJ stated that I was giving non-narcotics medication because the writer through the complaint was writing about Tylenol as narcotic, which is non-narcotic. The writer did not know what was narcotic. The ALJ stated that I was not checking the MAPS, even he stated in the PFD that he read a copy of MAPS in his nephew's chart and the ALJ did not know that checking MAPS means reading it on the State Website, nothing else was in the conclusion of Law.

The ALJ is excused because he is not a physician, he just took what was stated and put it in the PFD. The legislature requires that physicians should issue the final order after reviewing the PFD and the exceptions to PFD. It is clear that the Members of Disciplinary Subcommittee committed a crime when they voted on the devastating order without discussing the PFD and the Exceptions; **{Legal Felony}.**

LEGAL FELONY # 9 – The order of suspension my license was subject to judicial review. I filed an appeal in the Court of Appeals. The appeal took 18 months, while Mr. Hudson refused to respond to motion stay order pending appeal by grant, deny or saying anything in violation of the Law. He had to decide the motion anyway because the Court of Appeals could not decide the motion if it was not decided first by Mr. Hudson. This act is obstruction of justice. The suspension was for six months while the Appeal without staying the order took 18 months. Mr. Hudson is immune; **{Legal Felony}.**

LEGAL FELONY # 10 – Mr. Hudson filed a frivolous opposition to my application for reinstatement of my license so that the application go through hearing to delay the decision, it supposed to be done within 90 days, but it took more than 11 months. This is obstruction of justice; **{Legal Felony}.**

LEGAL FELONY # 11 – Mr. Hudson and Jessica Taub, both Assistant Attorney Generals prepared documents to contain forgery and entered them into evidence in the hearing. Preparing and presenting false evidence in a judicial proceeding to prejudice person is a felony. They are immune; **{Legal Felony}.**

LEGAL FELONY # 12 – During the hearing, Jessica Taub stated to the ALJ that since I had appealed the original order suspended my license; I did not admit my mistakes, so I was not eligible for reinstatement of the license. Retaliation for practicing legal right is illegal; **{Legal Felony}.**

LEGAL FELONY # 13 – I filed motion open record and remove false documents, Jessica Taub after she failed to respond to the motion; instead of removing the false documents she practiced pressure and bribed my attorney to make me withdraw the motion. Because my attorney business specialized in physicians' licenses, he would lose his business if he helped me, so I retired him from my case; **{Legal Felony}.**

LEGAL FELONY # 14 – Administrative Law Judge, Peter Plummer, after Jessica Taub failed to respond to my motion remove false documents, returned the motion for the record was closed in violation of law to cover Jessica Taub's crime. This act is obstruction of justice; **{Legal Felony}.**

LEGAL FELONY # 15 – The ALJ, Peter Plummer recommended deny reinstatement of my License based on that I appealed the original order. It is illegal retaliation for practicing my legal rights. Because he was immune, he stated that openly on an official document without fear or shame; **{Legal Felony}.**

LEGAL FELONY # 16 – Bill Schuette, the State Attorney General, I filed to him complaint twice, and I stated that I was calling from the underwater requesting investigation of multiple crimes or prosecute me for defamation. The Attorney General ignored both of my complaints. His gross negligence was the direct cause of most of the damages and obstruction of justice; **{Legal Felony}.**

LEGAL FELONY # 17 – The Board of Medicine voted on order extended the suspension and adopted PFD that was based only on a false document and illegal statement that deny reinstatement for I appealed the original order. They intentionally deprived me my freedom and property without due process of Law in violation of the Constitutions; **{Legal Felony}.**

CHAPTER 20

Michigan Court of appeals' order

◆ ◆ ◆

WHILE THE ORDER SUSPENDED LICENSE six months was pending in this appeal, the Board of Medicine issued a new order denying reinstatement of the license that extended the suspension to be for years. The Court of Appeals did not have jurisdiction on the new order that superseded the order subject of the appeal. The new order should be appealed to the Circuit Court then after the Circuit Court decision; it would come to the Court of Appeals in new appeal and a new season more than two years.

The Board of Medicine killed or hijacked the Appeal before its deciding. The pending Michigan Court of Appeals' order that I waited 18 months became useless. Winning was equal to losing. So I went to the Federal Court because it was the only option available. The Federal Court had dismissed the case for it did not have jurisdiction on the case for it was stated interest, and the defendants were shielded against suing by the absolute quasi-judicial Immunity doctrine.

Finally, the Court of Appeals' decision is next. Concerning the court order I have some comments on the order, but only I am presenting one comment, and I refer to (Chapter No. 11, Proposal for Decision and Chapter No. 12, My Exceptions to Proposal for Decision). The Court stated:

> *"Respondent opines that Hopper's information was inaccurate or misleading but offers nothing more than his own opinion in support of that argument. However, the fact that respondent disagreed with Hopper's testimony did not render it either untruthful or inadmissible. Rather, the conflict between the two was to be resolved by the fact-finder, which is invested with the authority to assess witness credibility".*

In my Exception to the PFD, I presented copies from three textbooks to prove that they committed perjury under oath and I shipped these books to Mr. Hudson. Notarized copies of selected pages from the three books were attached to my Exceptions and my Appellant Brief in the Court record. Moreover, I did not need evidence. Dr. Hopper told the ALJ that I was giving his nephew 10 mg Hydrocodone and 10 mg Hydrocodone is equal to 750 mg Morphine. Any person knows, or he can know from the internet that 10 mg is equivalent to 10 mg. Dr. Hopper told ALJ that I gave his nephew 1 mg Xanax a day and 1 mg Xanax is the maximum dose, while every person knows that there are tablets of Xanax 2 mg and 3 mg, and the maximum daily dose is 10 mg and could be more in case of emergency.

The Court of Appeals threw the ball back to the Fact Finder (the Board of Medicine). The Board of Medicine failed to review my Exceptions and three motions about this perjury in violation of the law. I filled appeal to resolve this problem. Now the Court of Appeals states it did not have the authorities to assess the credibility of the witness. What was the Judicial Review for if otherwise?

The state of Michigan
Court of Appeals

Docket No. 330222, April 25, 2017

DEPARTMENT OF LICENSING AND REGULATORY AFFAIRS, Board of Medicine

Petitioner-Appellee,

ABDELBASET ABDELMAGID YOUSSEF,

Respondent-Appellant.

Before: O'**Brien**, P.J., and **Servitto** and **Stephens,** JJ.

Per Curiam.

Respondent appeals by right the order issued by the Board of Medicine suspending his license to practice medicine for six months and a day, rendering void his license to prescribe controlled substances, and imposing a $20,000 fine, to be paid before he could apply for reinstatement of his medical license. We affirm.

I. FACTS AND PROCEDURAL HISTORY

Petitioner filed a two-count administrative complaint against respondent alleging negligence and incompetence under MCL 333.16221(a) and (b)(i), respectively, in part on the basis of data petitioner obtained from the Michigan Automated Prescriptions System (MAPS) indicating that respondent had prescribed more than 25,000 controlled substances between August 1, 2012, and July 31, 2013. Petitioner's complaint focused on four of respondent's patients, BS, AR, CH, and KB, and alleged that in each case he had issued monthly prescriptions for commonly abused controlled substances without offering the patients alternative treatments or monitoring them for abuse or diversion of the drugs. Petitioner's investigation was prompted when BS's mother, a retired nurse, found him in possession of a large number of drugs that had been prescribed by respondent and in a condition that led her to believe he had overdosed on drugs.

John Hopper, a licensed physician with expertise in opioid use, management, and dependence, testified that he reviewed these four patients' charts and MAPS reports and concluded that respondent's prescribing practices fell below the standard of care. Hopper's report to that effect was entered into evidence. Respondent testified that the amounts and combinations of medications he prescribed were necessary because his patients all suffered from conditions that caused chronic pain, which was often accompanied by anxiety and difficulty sleeping.

In the proposal for decision (PFD), the ALJ concluded that petitioner established that respondent violated MCL 333.16221(a) and (b)(i) by failing "to consider the use of other treatment modalities or non-narcotic medications for the treatment of pain," failing "to consistently monitor for abuse and diversion by utilizing urine drug testing and checking patients' prescription records with MAPS," and "prescribing an inappropriate combination of medication" Respondent filed exceptions to the PFD. The Board of Medicine's disciplinary subcommittee accepted the PFD after reviewing the record.

II. ANALYSIS

All final decisions, findings, rulings and orders of any administrative officer or agency existing under the constitution or by law, which is judicial or quasi-judicial and affects private rights or licenses, shall be subject to direct review by the courts as provided by law. This review shall include, as a minimum, the determination whether such final decisions, findings, rulings, and orders are authorized by law; and, in cases in which a hearing is required, whether the same are supported by competent, material and substantial evidence on the whole record, [Const. 1963, art 6, § 28.]

We "review the entire record and not just the portions supporting the agency's findings." *Dep't of Community Health v Risch,* 274 Mich. App. 365, 372; 733 NW2d 403 (2007). "Substantial evidence is evidence that a reasonable person would accept as sufficient to support a conclusion. While this requires more than a scintilla of evidence, it may be substantially less than a preponderance." *Id.* (quotation marks and citation omitted).

Motion to Dismiss

Respondent argues that the complaint should have been summarily dismissed. He alleged that the complaint did not state a claim under MCL 333.16221(a) or MCL 333.16221(b) (i). This is analogous to a motion under MCR 2.116(C) (8) which "tests the legal sufficiency of the claim on the pleadings alone to determine whether the plaintiff has stated a claim on which relief may be granted." *Spiek v Dep't of Transp.,* 456 Mich. 331, 337; 572 NW2d 201 (1998). "The motion must be granted if no factual development could justify the plaintiff's claim for relief." *Id.*

In this case, the tribunal ruled that the facts regarding respondent's record of prescribing drugs alleged in the complaint, "if proven, likely would be sufficient to establish a violation under MCL 333.16221(a) and (b) (i)" We agree. The factual assertion in the complaint cites the number of prescriptions for each of the named patients, the inappropriate combinations of such drugs and the lack of any record of the patients being advised about the dangers of the drugs or advice on alternative treatments. The complaint also states that the patients denied receiving such advice and counsel. This factual scenario adequately states a claim for violation of the cited laws.

Expert Testimony

Hopper's testimony was highly significant in this case, and the respondent argues that it should not have been admitted. The crux of his objections to Hopper's testimony concerns its veracity and scientific reliability. Hopper testified that respondent had prescribed KB a combination of hydrocodone, alprazolam, promethazine with codeine, Lorazepam, Butalbital, and Carisoprodol. Hopper stated that it "would be hard to imagine a patient receiving this combination of drugs and functioning at all," and that the combination could cause "sedation, confusion," and could "certainly result in death as well." Hopper noted that respondent continued to prescribe KB a stimulant that was known to increase a person's blood pressure, despite the fact that KB's blood pressure was "over two hundred," which Hopper stated was "shocking."

Hopper testified that respondent had not met the minimum standard of care for BS either, noting that BS's prescriptions would cause a person to be "sedated and not functional." Hopper stated that if a person were receiving "that many prescriptions and was functioning right," he would suspect that the person was not taking them, causing concern that they were being shared or sold to other people.

Respondent raises several arguments that are based largely on his assertion that Hopper's testimony contained incorrect information. Because he argued against the admission of some of this evidence at the hearing, we will consider this issue preserved. We are left to speculate the exact nature of his specific objections to portions of Hooper's testimony because they are addressed without transcript references. In general, we note that the admissibility of evidence in an administrative hearing is governed not by the Michigan Rules of Evidence but by the "somewhat relaxed" standard set forth in MCL 24.275. *Becker-Witt v Bd of Examiners of Social Workers,* 256 Mich. App. 359, 365; 663 NW2d 514 (2003). Respondent opines that Hooper's information was inaccurate or misleading but offers nothing more than his own opinion in support of that argument. However, the fact that respondent disagreed with Hopper's testimony did not render it either untruthful or inadmissible. Rather, the conflict between the two was to be resolved by the fact-finder, which is invested with the authority to assess witness credibility, *Risch,* 274 Mich. App at 372, and to weigh the evidence presented, *Surman v Surman,* 277 Mich. App. 287, 309; 745 NW2d 802 (2007).

Procedural Arguments

Respondent alleges errors concerning certain actions taken, or not taken, by petitioner with regard to the filing of the complaint, predicated on the applicable statutes. Respondent argues petitioner violated MCL 333.16228 by failing to have its complaint reviewed and approved by a controlled prescription panel before it was filed. MCL 333.16228 provides as follows:

(1) For an investigation involving the prescription of a controlled substance, the department *may* establish an ad hoc review panel to provide the department with expert information regarding a specific health profession or health specialty or a specific health care treatment

or procedure as it relates to the investigation. The department shall establish an ad hoc review panel under this subsection as follows:

A - The department shall triennially establish a pool of 10 physicians, 5 of, who are allopathic physicians licensed under part 170 [MCL 333.17001 *et* seq.] and 5 of whom are osteopathic physicians licensed under part 175 [MCL 333.17501 *et seq.].*

For each ad hoc review panel, the department shall appoint three physicians from the pool established under subdivision (a).

(2) The ad hoc review panel shall provide the information described in subsection (1) to the department during the investigation process and before a formal complaint is issued. [Emphasis added.]

In using the permissive "may" when speaking to the department's authority to establish an ad hoc review panel, thee Legislature clearly gave the department discretion to establish such a panel. See *People v Brown,* 249 Mich. App. 382, 386; 642 NW2d 382 (2002) ("The statutory term 'may' is permissive . . . ."). The correlating authority is the discretion not to establish such a panel. It is only when the department has exercised its discretion to establish an ad hoc review panel that MCL 333.16228 limits the department's authority. See *id.* ("[T]he terms 'shall' . . . carries a mandatory, nondiscretionary connotation.").

Respondent also argues that the complaint should have been reviewed by a person in the medical field before it was filed. However, he cites no authority in support. *Houghton v Keller,* 256 Mich. App. 336, 339-340; 662 NW2d 854 (2003). In any event, MCL 333.16231(6)(a) gives the department the authority to issue a formal complaint if an investigation indicates that a licensee has violated Article 15 of the Public Health Code, MCL 333.16101 through 333.18838. This section contains no requirement that the complaint is reviewed by a person with medical qualifications prior to filing.

Other Evidentiary Issues

Respondent made several other evidentiary arguments, again without specific transcript references. The arguments concern admission of evidence that was irrelevant to or outside the scope of the complaint as it was filed. Again, the admissibility of evidence in an administrative hearing is governed by the standard set forth in MCL 24.275. *Becker-Witt,* 256 Mich. App. At 365. However, even if respondent's characterization is accurate, the tribunal was not required to exclude irrelevant evidence under MCL 24.275. Further, the tribunal acknowledged that it had taken testimony that went outside the scope of the allegations set forth in the complaint, but it made it clear it would not consider that evidence when rendering a decision.

Respondent also argues that the tribunal admitted petitioner's exhibits before he had time to review them. However, the record reflects that respondent was offered the opportunity to review petitioner's exhibits at a pretrial conference and declined

Affirmed

/s/ Colleen A. O'Brien /s/ Deborah A. Servitto /s/ Cynthia Diane Stephens

CHAPTER 21

Hypocrisy of the Federal Legislature

◆ ◆ ◆

HYPOCRISY IN LEGISLATURE MEANS WHEN you read the Legislature it looks okay, but when it goes to practice in real life, it turned to be entirely different, due to hidden bomb inserted inside the legislature itself or mines planted in its road to the real life make it functionless.

An example of the hidden bomb inserted inside the legislature is the Egyptian Emergency Law. It makes the maximum period of the illegal arrest 45 days, which is acceptable in a third world country, but in real life, they arrest people for years because the legislature did not restrict the numbers of the illegal arrests.

An example of the road mines is the Federal Legislature, 42 U.S.C. 1983. It is excellent protection against the state tyrants, but in the road to the court, you will be stopped by many road bombs, such as Younger Abstention, Rooker-Feldman and the Absolute Quasi-judicial Immunity legal doctrines that make the Legislature functionless.

The only function of this kind of legislatures is to tell people worldwide that we have a decent legal system like any civilized country. So these laws are for export only, they are not for domestic use. The legislature gives something on the daylight and takes it in the darkness.

UNITED STATES CONSTITUTION; AMENDMENT XIV

Section 1:

All persons born or naturalized in the United States, and subject to the jurisdiction thereof, are citizens of the United States and of the state wherein they reside. No state shall make or enforce any law which shall abridge the privileges or immunities of citizens of the United States; nor shall any state deprive any person of life, liberty, or property, without due process of law; nor deny to any person within its jurisdiction the equal protection of the laws.

FEDERAL LEGISLATURE, 42 U.S.C. 1983

Every person who, under color of any statute, ordinance, regulation, custom, or usage, of any State or Territory or the District of Columbia, subjects, or causes to be subjected, any citizen of the United States or other person within the jurisdiction thereof to the deprivation of any rights, privileges, or immunities secured by the Constitution and laws, shall be liable to the party injured in an action at law, suit in equity, or other proper proceeding for redress, except that in any action brought against a judicial officer for an act or omission taken in such officer's judicial capacity, injunctive relief shall not be granted unless a declaratory decree was violated or declaratory relief was unavailable. For this section, any Act of Congress applicable exclusively to the District of Columbia shall be considered to be a statute of the District of Columbia.

The people of North Korea, if they had read this Constitution Article XIV and the Legislature 42 USC 1983, they would be jealous of American people for this kind of luxury protection. However the matter is not just good Constitution or Legislature, North Korea may have excellent Constitution as well. The Constitution and Legislature are only pieces of paper if there are no powers translate them into real thing on the ground. This power is an executive authority controlled by a court.

Like the North Koreans, I read the Constitution; Amendment XIV and the 42 U.S.C. 1983 and when the State Officials suspended my license for years without due process of law, and I lost my assets, and my life was ruined, and thousands of my patients were injured. I believed that the Federal Court is the power that makes the Constitution and Legislature real on the ground.

I escaped to the Federal Court. I found its door was locked by four enormous English Steel Locks. I had to break all of the four locks to get help. Even I was able to cut the first bolt; I could not even touch any one of the other three latches. The Constitution did not work for me; I could not enjoy the Constitutional protection, so I am not happier than my North Korean friends. Only the great people of America, who made the Constitution, can break all of these locks and salvage the great Constitution of the United States of America.

The Michigan Attorney General and the Board of Medicine, through two quasi-judicial proceedings (physician disciplinary proceedings), deprived me of life, liberty, and property without due process of law. I went to the Federal Court, the Eastern District of Michigan in case no. 17-cv-10610.

First lock: Constitution, Amendment XI immunizes the State and the State agencies against suing in the Federal Court:

US Constitution; Amendment XI: The judicial power of the United States shall not be construed to extend to any suit in law or equity, commenced or prosecuted against one of the United States by citizens of another state, or by citizens or subjects of any foreign state.

I was able to break this lock by amending my complaint, where I removed the state agencies as defendants and kept only the individual defendants in the complaint as they were not immune by the Amendment XI.

Second Lock: *Younger Abstention Doctrine*; this legal doctrine did not allow suing in the Federal Court for claims included state interest or claims pending in a state court proceeding. Physician disciplinary proceeding is stated interest and the first order of suspension of my medical license six months, at that time, was pending in the Michigan Court of Appeals. I could not touch this lock. Theoretically, even If I was able to break this lock, there were still two more locks to be cut to go through the Court door.

Third Lock: *Rooker-Feldman Doctrine* is legal doctrine did not allow the Federal District Court to review the State Court final decisions.

I had some claims escaped from the second lock (Younger Abstention) as they were not pending in any state court; one of these claims was the second board of medicine's order that extended the suspension of the license from 6 months to be for years. The Michigan Court of Appeals had not had jurisdiction on this new order that supersedes the original order pending in it. Since the state court lost its jurisdiction on the extension of the suspension, the suspension became out of the control of the state court, and accordingly, it became final, so it escaped from the second lock {Younger Abstention).

Unfortunately; the Third Lock (Rooker-Feldman Doctrine) did not allow the Federal Court to review the state court's final decisions. So the claims that escaped the Younger Abstention could not escape Rooker-Feldman doctrine. So I could not break the third lock as well. All of my claims were either pending or final; thus all of them were barred by Younger Abstention and Rooker-Feldman doctrines. By common sense, if the claim is not pending it is final, and if it is not final it is pending. Like chicken and egg. All of my claims were some chickens and some eggs. There is no place for either chickens or eggs in the federal court.

Forth Lock: *The Absolute Quasi-judicial Immunity*: Even I did not need to break this lock because breaking it was useless anyway, as I could not break the previous two Locks. However since this lock is the subtitle of this book, I need to mention it.

All of the individual defendants, who were state officials and employees, were absolutely immune against suing in any federal or state court for damages resulted from their felonies because they did all of their felonies about a quasi-judicial proceeding (physician disciplinary proceeding). This immunity was established by the absolute quasi-judicial immunity doctrine.

I do not know when the 42 U.S.C. 1983 will be active to do its protection job. What kind of claim against the state could we sue it for in the Federal Court? All of the States deprive their people of life, liberty or property without due process through quasi-legal proceedings. By common sense, any claim is either pending in a state court and agency or final, either way, is barred by Younger or Rooker-Feldman. All of the claims against the state were made by a state agency which is immune by Amendment XI or individuals who are shielded by absolute quasi-judicial immunity. It is very clear that 42 U.S.C 1983 cannot do the protection that it was issued for, so it is functionless, and the USA Constitution Amendment XIV has been suspended for good.

I called my North Korean friends and told them: do not be jealous any more, as we are in the same condition, what you read in the US Constitution Art. XIV and Legislature 42 USC 1983 is not

functioning anymore because they are not usable outside a federal court, while Mr. Younger, Mr. Feldman, and the Quasi-judicial Immunity have locked all of the Federal Courts for good. Mr. Kim Jong-un can deprive you of life for any reason without due process of law, my State Officials had deprived me of life, liberty, and property without due process of law as well, but I could not sue them in any federal or state court because they are absolutely immune like Mr. Kim Jong-un

CHAPTER 22

Complaint in Detroit Federal Court

◆ ◆ ◆

IT WAS THE FIRST TIME to know about the Absolute Quasi-judicial Immunity of the State Officials was through my complaint in the Federal Court. I had believed that all crimes were illegal. It had never come to my mind that in specific situations the felony could be legally protected.

During the two hearings in the Administrative Hearing System, I was amazed to see people committing crimes such as obstruction of justice and perjury under oath, naked without fear or shame. They were not making any effort to hide their crimes as we used to see in case of the regular unimmunized illegal crimes. I felt it was amazing because I believed the state officials and employees were unarmored like regular people.

I filed an appeal with full confidence in winning. I expected a lot of arrests and prosecutions. While the appeal of the original order was pending in the Court of Appeals, state officials issued a new order denying reinstatement of my license. I filed a supplemental brief in the Court of Appeals might consider the new order extended the suspension for good along with the original order subject of the Appeal. The Court returned the Brief for it had not had jurisdiction over the new order. The Appeal was killed or hijacked before it was decided. So the appellees won the appeal from their office. What kind of law was this?

Court of Appeals, State of Michigan

ORDER

In re Abdelbaset Abdelmagid Youssef MD

Docket No. 330222 LC No. 15-015505

Michael F. Gadola, Judge, acting under MCR 7.211(E)(2) orders: 1 - The motion for immediate consideration of the motion to strike appellee's answer is GRANTED.

2 - The motion to strike appellee's answer is DENIED.

3 - The motion to file a supplemental brief filed on February 3, 2017, is DENIED. Thus, the Clerk's Office is directed to return the proposed second supplemental brief submitted with that motion to appellant without accepting it for filing.

The new order superseded the original order, subject of the appeal and the Court of Appeals had not had jurisdiction over it. The pending appeal had become dead, or in legal language, it is called moot. This means winning the appeal equal to losing it. The State Officials hijacked the appeal by issuing new superseding order outside the reach of the Court of Appeals.

The only option available to me was the Federal Court. On 2/27/2017 I filed a complaint in the Federal Court. I amended the complaint on April 18, 2017.

UNITED STATES DISTRICT COURT

EASTERN DISTRICT OF MICHIGAN

AMENDED COMPLAINT, F. R. CIVL 15(a) (1) (B)

Declaratory, Injunctive, and Compensatory and punitive reliefs
Case: 2:17-cv-10610 HON. VICTORIA A. ROBERTS
MAG. DAVID R. GRAND
Abdelbaset Abdelmagid Youssef

Plaintiff

Vs.

1 – Bill Schuette; Attorney General of the State of Michigan.
2 – Dennis Szymanski, M.D., member of the Board of Medicine.
3 – Robert Regan, R. Ph. Investigator; witness for LARA.
4 – Andrew Hudson, Assistant Attorney General at LARA
5 – Jessica Taub, Assistant Attorney General, at LARA.
6– John Hopper M.D. works at LARA and its Expert witness.
7 – Peter Graham, M.D., Chairperson of the Board of Medicine.
8 – Kim Gaedeke, Director Bureau of Professional Licensing

Defendants

I -Statement of Jurisdiction

1 - This Court has original Jurisdiction on the matter by U.S. Constitution Amendment XIV, part 1, 28 U.S.C. 1331, 28 U.S.C. 2201, 28 U.S.C. 2202, and supplemental jurisdiction by Michigan Constitution article 1, section 17 and Michigan Legislature.

II - Declaration and Affidavit;

I, Abdelbaset A Youssef, Pro Se plaintiff, in this case, certify that I am over 18 years and competent to give the following declaration and affidavits.

A - All the statements and exhibits I presented and I will present, included in this case or anywhere related to this case are true to my best knowledge.

B – I came to the Federal Court, only after the State Officials have violated the laws to lock the State Court System so that no court in the state could give any functioning relief in a typical case of obstruction of justice. During discovery, I will have a chance to show how violation of the laws locked the State Court System.

C – I am not able to bring all of the facts because most of the relevant evidence is in the custody of the defendants. I strongly need discovery to be able to found my claims. I need testimonies from defendants and Board of Medicine's members.

D – During discovery, I will have chances to bring the records and transcripts of the infringed hearings from the defendants and have a chance to get statements and many more resources to found my claims. I may need expert witnesses.

E –The State Court System is completely locked. No state court could reinstate my License. The only hope is the Federal Court; if this complaint were dismissed no hope to be back to my profession. For I did nothing wrong. Subsequently escalated retaliations were just for personal conflict and practicing my legal rights ruined my life and injured thousands of patients.

F – Legal Immunity was invented to help justice. It is not to facilitate crimes.

III - Authorities

1 - US Constitution: Article XIV (Amendment 14 - Rights Guaranteed: Privileges and Immunities of Citizenship, Due Process, and Equal Protection)

All persons born or naturalized in the United States, and subject to the jurisdiction thereof, are citizens of the United States and the State wherein they reside. No State shall make or enforce any law which shall abridge the privileges or immunities of citizens of the United States; nor shall any State deprive any person of life, liberty, or property, without due process of law; nor deny to any person within its jurisdiction the equal protection of the laws.

2 – Michigan Constitution: Article I § 17 Self-incrimination; due process of law; fair treatment at investigations.

Sec.17. No person shall be compelled in any criminal case to be a witness against himself, nor be deprived of life, liberty or property, without due process of law. The right of all individuals, firms, corporations and voluntary associations to fair and just treatment in the course of legislative and executive investigations and hearings shall not be infringed.

IV – Facts of the Compliant.

1 – I am a physician had been practicing medicine for 30 years, the last ten years I dedicated them to treating only patients with chronic pain syndrome along with other medical problems. At least 80% of my patients were officially considered disable.

2 - In early 2014, defendant, no: 2, Mr. Regan came to my office. He asked if I own the office building and how much rent I was collecting from Farmor pharmacy in my building. He told me to do not allow Friendly pharmacy put flyers in the waiting room. He told me that a lady complained that her son B.S. who had a history of work accident caused herniated Lumbar Disc and spinal stenosis, for I was giving him narcotics while he can control his pain by Motrin. He collected a copy of about, randomly selected, 30 patients' charts.

3 – On 9/18/2014, Mr. Hudson filed the complaint. Since it was in pain management, I did not expect the writer did not know the basics

of medicine. The writer, through the complaint, was writing about Tylenol as the controlled medicine. When I filed answer, I claimed that the writer was doing fraud. Only after seven months, on 4/23/2015, during the hearing, I had known that the writer was Mr. Hudson, where we entered in a personal conflict, (The complaint is Exhibit no. A).

4 – On November 2014, I was investigated by Rosalie Tocco Bradley, M.D., Ph.D. consultant of pain management and member of the Board of Medicine. In the presence of Mr. Hudson, she stated that I was seeing very sick people and I was doing well.

5 – On 11/4/2014, Mr. Hudson had sent to me offer for settlement, among its conditions I had to pay $5000 fine. I refused to pay if they did not say what wrong I did. I requested hearing to get relief.

6 – On 4/23/2015, during the hearing, everything is recorded in the transcript. Mr. Hudson gave me a stack of about 600 pages/papers and asked me to read and admit in 5 minutes. The ALJ entered and asked me if I admitted these papers, I told him I cannot admit; I do not know them. I need to read them at home. Even I stated that the ALJ stated that they were admitted.

7 - On 4/23/2015, during the hearing, the ALJ told Mr. Hudson, he noticed one of the witnesses was his cousin. Mr. Hudson said: yeas Judge, she is and he added; she is the complainant for her son, B.S. as well.

8 - The mother of patient B.S. the complainant and the first witness; she stated that her son lost weight because he had trouble with his wife, who left home and had five children from 3 women, has back pain, so he was not eating well. While the original Complaint stated that I was liable for his weight loss, the PFD Fact no. 27 considered

me liable as well. She stated that he has a history of alcohol abuse and she found him drunk. She stated that she found two bottles of Vicodin and Atarax carrying my name, while I have not prescribed single tablet of these two medications, brand name or generic or under any name. Defendants know, and they cannot dispute, if I prescribed any of these medications, as they have B.S.' chart and MAPS.

9 – Witness Robert Regan, R. Ph. Works in LARA:-

A – During the hearing, on 4/23/2015, he testified clear lies outside the scope of the allegations of the complaint to mislead the ALJ.

B – (PFD, finding facts no. 7 – 11), he stated: because respondent's patients in the market for Diversion, they have to go far to get the pharmacy that dispenses their prescriptions, so they aggregate in pharmacies mostly far away, at Bellavista, Pharmor, Friendly and Knight Drug Pharmacies.

The first Pharmacy was cross street from my office at 388 Inkster Rd, Inkster MI 48141. The second one was inside my office. When he came, he asked me how much rent I was collecting from it. The third one is close to my office so that he saw its flyers in the waiting room and asked me to stop that.

C – He said that I prescribe Hydrocodone, while Dr. Honet (Pain Consultant) prescribes Morphine, while he knew at that time Hydrocodone was DEA schedule III and Morphine was II. We were allowed to give five refills for Schedule III, in one visit, but no refill for Morphine. He tried to make the ALJ thinks Morphine is safer than Hydrocodone, as I was giving Hydrocodone to the ALJ's relative. All of these are lies outside the scope of the complaint added to the PFD.

10 – Since Mr. Regan is a Pharmacist, I believed, he wrote the complaint, I asked him about the defects in the complaint. Mr. Hudson got

angry and accused me that I knew that he, who wrote it as his name, who signed it. He believed I was trying to defame him. He stated: he did that because the subject is outside his experience.

11 - John Hopper, M.D., Expert Witness. He is defendant no. 6.

A – He was the expert witness in the hearing, on 4/23/2015. He was spraying lies without any kind of restrictions. He testified lies not only in the subjects related to the complaint but also subjects not related to the complaint. He testified lies about A.R. Asthma and COPD; I filed Motion to the ALJ for his testimonies are lies and outside scope of the complaint. He filed report included three unknown patients, who were not in the complaint. The report contains lies as well.

B – He was not qualified to testify as expert witness in chronic pain management case, as he has never treated a single case of pain management in a primary care setting.

C – I filed three motions to exempt him from being an expert witness and exempt his testimony and his report. My motions were denied for untimely.

D – Examples of his lies; respondent was giving B.S. (ALJ's relative) 10 mg Hydrocodone, then 10 mg Hydrocodone is equal to 750 mg Morphine. Any textbook from Tokyo to New York says 10 mg Hydrocodone equal to 10 mg oral Morphine or 3.3 mg injectable Morphine. Another lie, the maximum dose of Xanax is 1 mg, while there are tablets of Xanax 3 mg. The maximum daily dose is 10 mg, could be more in case of emergency. (PFD facts: 15-20). Most of his testimonies were lies and outside the scope of the complaint.

11 – The witnesses directed their grave lies about patient B.S, the ALJ's relative. They drew scenario as if I almost kill him. To make the ALJ loses his impartiality.

12 – Lies were in the PFD; I answered them in my Exceptions to the PFD. I supported my answers in my Exceptions to the PFD with copies from 3 standard textbooks. Even I shipped the three textbooks to Mr. Hudson. I answered each fact and each conclusion of law with indisputable evidence. Mr. Hudson has never disputed any of my evidence.

13 – Even though I had known that Mr. Hudson conspired with Mr. Regan and Dr. Hopper to fabricate infringed hearing, I felt that there was hope to be corrected in the Board of Medicine, Disciplinary Subcommittee. By Law, R 792.10131, they have to review my exceptions before the order became final.

R 792.10131. (3) A decision shall become a final decision in the absence of exceptions or review by an entity with final decision authority.

MCL 333.16237(3) In reviewing the recommended findings of fact and conclusions of law of the hearings examiner and the record of the hearing, a disciplinary subcommittee may request the hearings examiner to take additional testimony or evidence on a specific issue or may revise the recommended findings of fact and conclusions of law as determined necessary by the disciplinary subcommittee, or both.

14 – I was shocked by defendant no: 2, Dennis Szymanski, M.D., member of the Board of Medicine. He presented the final order for voting without reviewing my exceptions to the PFD as described by laws. Even he did not mention them.

15 – Discovery is required to know if Dr. Szymanski had intentionally ignored my Exceptions to the PFD or Mr. Hudson had never presented my Exceptions to the committee as a part of his retaliation plot.

16 – Even the final order of suspension my license minimum six months and $20,000 fine was entered on 10/30/2015, there was great

hope. By MCL 333.16241 and MCL 333.16237, the final order is subject to judicial review in the Court of Appeals. There was no doubt the Court will vacate the order. If the order were stayed there would be no damage. (Order Exhibit no. D).

17 - The allegations do not establish claims of violation of MCL 333.16221(a) and (b) (i).

The Allegations in the Complaint as follows:

A – Allegations no. 1 thru 12 is true, but they do not state claims.

B – Allegations no. 13, 14, 15, 17, 18, 21, 22, 23, 26, 27, 28, 29, 30, 31, 34, 36, and 38, Could be true but none of them establishes violations of MCL 333.16221(a) and (b)(i). The hearing officer did not claim that they establish violations as well, so I do not need to address them.

C – Allegations 19, 20, 24, 25, 32, 33, 35, 37, 39, and 40. All of them are summarized by the Allegation no. 16 items {a thru f}. Because the ALJ did not rule in items d thru f; I have to address only the items {a thru c}.

18 – Allegation 16 (a) Failure to consider the use of other treatment modalities or non-narcotic pain medications. Every patient in my office including these four patients has, at least, one non-narcotic pain medicine in each visit. Regarding other modalities, the main subject of discussion during the visit every visit for each patient is considering other modalities. No one in this four patient; candidate for other modality, patient B.S. left my office since 2012; his mother testified positively that he has never received physical therapy or other modality for pain. In my exceptions I asked the Petitioner may assign one patient, who needed other modality but I deprived him. I presented copies from the standard textbook of pain management, show that I was doing the

same as the books and I asked the Petitioner to bring any textbook say otherwise.

19 – Allegation 16(b), Failure to consistently monitor for abuse and diversion by urine drug test or MAPS. For the last ten years, I see only patients who have chronic pain. No doctor could work in pain management without monitoring for abuse or diversion. PFD finding fact no. 13 states that I was monitoring by MAPS. If I do not monitor, how the four patients MAPS are clean? Patient B.S. had few times small amounts of controlled medicine from the ER. The pain contract that every patient is authorized to get help from the E.R. The petitioner's expert witness agreed that shortage of pain medicine could put the patient in the risk of death (Transcript p.116 lines 10-17). Patient K.B. had duplicated three prescriptions in 2011 because she did not know Ativan and Xanax belong to the same family of medicine.

I check the MAPS every visit, but I do not print it if it is O.K. as there is no need for counseling. No guideline or Statue or recommendation mandates printing the MAPS or Urine Drug test result even if it is OK.

20 – Allegation 16 (c) prescribing an inappropriate combination of medication. In any textbook; standard treatment for chronic back pain syndrome secondary to structural damage in the spinal cord is pain medicine + Muscle relaxant + Antianxiety, Narcotics and Soma and Xanax all are approved by the FDA either in combination or separate. Xanax is approved as the first line of treatment for pain-related anxiety. In my Exceptions, I discussed that and presented copies of textbooks to support my statement and asked the petitioner to present any textbook states otherwise.

21 - The agency's decision is not supported by competent material and substantial evidence in the whole record.

22 – On 11/13/2015, I filed a claim of Appeal and motion for a stay order. The Court of Appeals denied staying because *MCR 7.209(2) motion for bond or a stay pending appeal may not be filed in the Court of Appeals unless such a motion was decided by the trial court.*

23 – On 11/25/2015, I filed a motion to stay on the Board of Medicine. Mr. Hudson, who was in charge of the case as an attorney to the Board has never answered the motion to deprive the Court of Appeals Jurisdiction on the matter of stay in a typical case of obstruction of Justice.

24 – I filed the motion three times in the Court of Appeals, every time Mr. Hudson says he never received my motion to the Board. In the last time, I presented evidence of delivery to him. He confessed that he received it put he considered it a motion for reconsideration. The Court denied the motion. By that time the six-month suspension was about to finish, so it was better to concentrate on reinstatement.

25 – It does not make sense; the order was a suspension for six months, while the order without a stay, the court reviews it, after 18 months. The order should be automatically stayed by filing an appeal, or expedited appeal gives relief in a reasonable time, or they should not offer a chance for appeal, in the first place.

26 – On 2/11/2016, I filed a complaint with Mr. Hudson's supervisor, (Mr. Bill Schuette, the State Attorney General). I stated: Mr. Andrew Hudson, AAG, have been conspiring with Mr. Robert Regan R. Ph., and Hopper M.D., to subject me to severe cycles of torture as retaliation for personal conflict, requesting to investigate the situation or keep them away from my business to save me from deadly stress.

I requested if he may investigate the situation to relieve me from deadly stress as I was admitted twice in 2 hospitals for cardiac issues related to this kind of strange stress or he may change him by another AAG. Mr. Schuette has never answered any of my complaints.

27 – If Mr. Bill Schuette did not neglect his duty and interfered in the matter, on time, he would save me from obstruction of justice and make court system work properly. If Mr. Hudson were changed, by another AAG, at least, my License would be reinstated on time that would save me from the greater part of the damage.

28 – After I lost hope for staying pending appeals, on 3/5/2016, I applied for reinstatement. Just one day before the end of the six-month suspension, Mr. Hudson had resumed his retaliation. He filed frivolous opposition claimed that I was not honest.

29 – On 7/5/2016, during a hearing for reinstatement of the license, Mr. Hudson conspired with defendant no: 5, Jessica Taub, AAG, to file fabricated documents.

30 - Defendant no: 5, Jessica Taub, Attorney at the hearing.

A – During the hearing, on 7/5/2016, she told the ALJ, that I was not eligible for reinstatement because; since I had filed Appeal I still did not admit my mistakes.

B – On 7/5/2016, during the hearing for reinstatement of my license before ALJ, Peter Plummer, she presented fabricated documents and witness who told lies under oath. She did this fraud to prove that I was not honest so that I would not be eligible for reinstatement.

C – I filed a motion to open the record and remove this document, as I presented evidence that it is false, but the ALJ, after she failed to answer the motion, returned it for the record was closed. By law, the ALJ should open the record and decided the motion. He held the motion until the deadline for response passed then he knew that she was not able to respond to my motion, so he returned it.

D – My Attorney's business is specialized in Physicians' Licenses, so his business is through them. I have evidence that she practiced pressure on him to make him force me to withdraw the motion, so I retired him.

30 – In PFD for reinstatement of my license, The ALJ said in the PFD finding facts 11 thru 14, due to the short period of suspension, he still claims that he was tricked by the Authorities when he committed an act of incompetence. ALJ recommended denying until I understand, as he stated. This is equal to; I am not hungry enough to give up my appeal. The order was suspension six months and one day, but now it became more than two years. It is illegal to use filing appeal as a condition for denying reinstatement; this is a criminal way to defend the Appeal. The Board of Medicine should defend the Appeal in the Court of Appeals.

31 – On 9/28/2016, I filed another complaint with Mr. Bill Schuette, State Attorney General, I stated: I, Abdelbaset A Youssef, M.D., hereby raise to your honor this complaint. Because of a personal conflict with Andrew Hudson Assistant Attorney General, he and Jessica Taub Assistant Attorney general have conspired with the Administrative Law Judge Peter Plummer to commit a grave crime against me. They illegally delayed reinstatement of my license, and they are going to deny it. They use hunger, to defend my Appeal that I filed on 11/13/2015, against their order on 10/30/2015, suspending my License, instead of using the legal way. Mr. Bill Schuette, State Attorney General, again ignored my complaint. Mr. Bill Schuette negligence of my complaints encouraged Mr. Hudson kept violating the laws. Mr. Bill Schuette negligence was considered a pardon or even approval of these acts.

31 - On 01/18/2017, the Board of Medicine approved order denying my application for reinstatement. By law, I cannot reapply for reinstatement before 01/18/2018. (Order denying reinstatement, Exhibit no. G).

33 – On 1/31/2017, I filed a supplemental brief in the Court of Appeals may consider the new order along with the original order subject of this Appeal and I stated that; the members of the Board of Medicine are very busy physicians from all over the State. Every two months, they visit Lansing for few hour Board meeting. On 9/16/2015, they reviewed full records and voted for 25 final decisions related to 25 physicians including myself in 94 minutes. One Assistant Attorney General does practically all the business of the Board. He writes the complaint then in the day, attorney for the Board of Medicine and at night he is the Judge, who issues the final Judgment. He is Attorney and Judge at the same time for the same case. There is no full-time M.D., dedicated to doing the exclusively medical business. (Supplemental Brief: Exhibit no. H), (Order returns brief, Exhibit no. I).

34 – The Court of Appeals has returned the brief as it had not had Jurisdiction over the new order. I have to appeal the new order in the Circuit Court. If the Circuit reversed the order, the Board of Medicine has a chance to appeal the Circuit Court's order to the Court of Appeals. The new season will take at least two more years.

35 – No one can say, in this situation, the State Court System can give any relief or has any control over the state officials. The Court of Appeals' pending opinion on the original Board of Medicine's order, suspending my License, is useless. I am sure, the Court will vacate the order subject of the appeal, but it cannot reinstate my license, so what I do by winning the appeal.

V - Summary of the Subject of the Complaint

36 - I am a physician, had practiced medicine for 30 years, my Medical License was suspended without due process of Law. Since 10/30/2015 – so far, I have not been working. I lost my medical practice that my family and I had built over 13 years.

37 - Due to a personal conflict with defendant no: 4, Mr. Hudson, he conspired with the defendants no: 3, Mr. Regan and 6, Dr. Hopper to infringe the hearing to issue order suspended my License minimum six months and $20,000 fine, in clear violation of the US Constitution Amendment XIV.

38 – This case is very complicated. The ALJ, he, said that he is related to the complainant witness. Otherwise, I would not know. The ALJ has nothing to do with the infringed hearing. He is not a physician. He just got what was stated and put it in PFD. The same thing on the Board of Medicine, Dr. Szymanski member of the Board, who presented the order for Disciplinary Subcommittee for voting without reviewing my Exceptions to PFD in violation of the law. Without discovery, it is not clear if Dr. Szymanski did that intentionally or because Mr. Hudson had failed to deliver my Exceptions to the Board of Medicine as a part of his retaliation plot.

39 - Mr. Hudson abused his authority as Attorney for the Board of Medicine to commit an illegal act to deprive me of staying order pending Appeal, the thing that deprived me of getting timely functioning relief from the Michigan Court of Appeals. He refused to answer my motion to stay neither by deny nor by grant in violation of MCL 24.304. He is individually responsible for these separate illegal acts, away from the Board of Medicine and has nothing to do with the order itself. He did that to deprive me of staying neither in the Board nor the Court of

Appeals. It is a typical case of obstruction of justice. (Suspension was for six months, while the appeal to get relief from it, without a stay, takes 18 months, even still I have to go to another Court. I need more than three years, without work, to get relief from 6 months suspension. In this situation, no one can claim that state court system gives any functioning relief.

40 - I filed complaint twice to defendant no: 1, Bill Schuette, State Attorney General, to investigate the case to stop Mr. Hudson, AAG, from torturing me or change him. I stated to Mr. Schuette that, because of a personal conflict, he has conspired with others to infringe the hearing and he kept retaliating so that I was admitted in 2 hospitals from the stress of feeling injustice. I sent a copy of the complaints to Mr. Hudson as well. Mr. Schuette had failed to answer any of my complaints the thing that had encouraged Mr. Hudson kept committing crimes of torturing and damaging in escalated manner. Mr. Hudson felt that he was pardoned. Even Mr. Hudson may felt that his acts were approved.

41 - Later Mr. Hudson conspired with defendant no: 5, Jessica Taub, during a hearing for reinstating of my license, she used fabricated documents and illegal statement to issue a new order extended the suspension of my license to be minimum two years. The Court of Appeals has no jurisdiction over the new order. I had to appeal the new order to the Circuit Court in a season takes at least two more years.

42 - By the time I would get relief from both orders. By Law, I will not be able to reinstate my license as I will be more than three years out of medical practice.

43 - If the order were stayed pending Appeal as per State's Law, defendants would not be able to issue the second order that blocked the state courts.

44 - I have filed this complaint to get declaratory relief, injunctive relief reinstates my license immediately, and compensatory and punitive relief from damages.

45 – Only after discovery everything became clearer regarding the role of each in this case. Any motion to dismiss without discovery is deniable.

VI - Conclusion

During discovery, I will have a chance to explore further and state more facts.

These defendants, who, I have sued in their individual capacity, cannot claim qualified immunity because they intentionally violated the law as follows:

46 – Mr. Hudson, AAG, (defendant no: 4), he cannot claim qualified immunity because he intentionally violated the laws as follows:

A – He wrote a defective complaint in a subject outside his experience that resulted in the personal conflict. MCL 333.16228, states that even regular physician cannot write a complaint in controlled medicine, so the Statue required that the controlled prescriptions panel should review this kind of complaints. A reasonable official in the position of Mr. Hudson would not write a complaint in medicine when it was outside his experience, or he does not know the basics of medicine. It is clear; that his act is gross negligence planted seeds for all of the damages.

B – Did Mr. Hudson, intentionally, select the ALJ conducting the hearing, who is a cousin of the complainant, mother of Patient B.S.? Or it was by accident. A chance to be by accident is less than 0.01%. The reasonable official in his position knows that intentional selection of ALJ's cousin complainant, witness, mother of the patient is illegal as it was for infringing the hearing in violation of the Constitutions

C – Did Mr. Hudson conspired with Mr. Regan and Dr. Hopper to commit grave lies about management of B.S., ALJ's relative? If he did not know that they were testifying lies, I filed to him my Exceptions to PFD stated with evidence that they testified lies, among this evidence three standard textbooks. A reasonable official in his position knows, even if he is not a physician, from this evidence that witnesses were testifying lies under oath.

D – After I filed a claim of Appeal, on 11/25/2015, I filed a motion to stay order in the Board of Medicine, as Mr. Hudson was in charge to be an Attorney to the Board; he got the original of the motion. He has never answered the motion neither denies nor grants or saying anything. A reasonable official knows no answer is a violation of MCL 24.304(1). He knows that no answer, due to MCR 7.209, deprive the Court of Appeals jurisdiction on the matter. He knows this act causes a great deal of damage and if the Court of appeals vacates the order after 18 months, its order will be valueless. Reasonable official knows that this act is gross negligence, intentional infliction of damage and obstruction of justice.

E – I filed recurrent motions to stay in the Court of Appeals, every time, on official documents he denied receiving it, only after I filed the evidence of delivery he confessed on opposition to my motion that he received it but he considered its motion for reconsideration. A reasonable official in this situation would not be confused between a motion for stay pending appeal and motion for reconsideration.

F – On 2/11/2016, I filed a complaint with Mr. Bill Schuette, State Attorney General, that Mr. Hudson, due to the personal conflict was targeting me, causing deadly stress. I mailed a copy to Mr. Hudson as well. The ethics require Mr. Hudson either recuse himself or states why he did not recuse himself.

47 – Discovery by testimony, will give me a chance to know if Dr. Szymanski intentionally violated the law when he presented the order for voting without reviewing my Exceptions to the PFD or Mr. Hudson had never delivered the Exceptions to the Board of Medicine, as a part of his plot.

Without discovery, I cannot know whether Dr. Szymanski or Mr. Hudson responsible for violation of the Laws R 792.10131 and MCL 333.16237.

Mr. Hudson's duty was to transfer the record of the case to the Disciplinary Subcommittee, where Dr. Szymanski reviewed the record. By-Laws, R 792.10131 and Law, MCL 333.16237, they have to review my exception before the order became final:

R 792.10131. (3) A decision shall become a final decision in the absence of exceptions or review by an entity with final decision authority and

MCL 333.16237(3) In reviewing the recommended findings of fact and conclusions of law of the hearings examiner and the record of the hearing, a disciplinary subcommittee may request the hearings examiner to take additional testimony or evidence on a specific issue or may revise the recommended findings of fact and conclusions of law as determined necessary.

48 – Mr. Bill Schuette, State Attorney General, neglected his duty when he neglected my complaint twice. He owes me a duty to protect me not only from his assistants but also from anybody else. He was able to save me from most of the damages if he acted on time. Reasonable State Attorney General knows that it is gross negligence, when he neglects complaints about one of his assistants, especially if

the complaint includes true threat for deadly risk and severely destructive damages may occur due to neglecting this duty. Mr. Hudson read or misread his supervisor neglect as pardon or approval of his acts. What is the duty of the State Attorney if otherwise? Mr. Hudson works in the name of the Attorney General.

49 – Discovery will give me a chance to get further proofs that Mr. Regan had testified lies under oath in conspiracy with Mr. Hudson. I will prove that he committed grave lies. A reasonable pharmacist knows that a pharmacy inside the same building with a medical office, cross the street from it, or 1.24 mile from it, is not considered far away from that office. He knows Narcotic DEA schedule II is not safer than Schedule III. Schedule III is safer so that we can give the patient up to 6 month supply in refills in one visit. We cannot give any refill for Schedule II. He did that along with many other lies in the hearing's transcript to attack the ALJ's impartiality, as he was testifying lies about management of ALJ's cousin's son.

50 – Dr. Hopper had been spraying lies under oath without restrictions. No reasonable physician or physician assistant, who does not know 10 mg Hydrocodone equal to 10 mg Morphine, not 750 mg or he knows the maximum dose of Xanax is not 1 mg, as there is tablet 3 mg Xanax. He told these lies to make the ALJ thinks as if I almost kill his cousin's son. Discovery will help me prove many more lies.

VII - Damages subject to the requested relief

51 – The infringed hearing and neglecting my exceptions that lead to order suspended my license and the actions that were done after the Board had issued this order, had destroyed my medical practice, the business that my family and I had built, over 13 years. The business

was Solo primary care medical practice, Internal Medicine/pain management, {Astoria Medical P C) at 4811 Venoy Rd. Wayne, Michigan 48184. Upon closing the practice, it had about six thousand files and 878 active patients, and I was the only doctor in it and the only owner of it. On 12/01/2015, to be compliant with the order, I stopped working and informed the patients that my license was suspended to find another office, but I kept the office open without seeing patients in hope Mr. Hudson might stay the order pending appeal. Ultimately I lost hope for staying the order, and the business was closed and dissolved for good. Every patient had found another primary care office. This business was everything to me. If my license were reinstated, I need at least 13 years to build one like it. (Exhibit no. J; Federal Tax Returns for 2013 to 2016). I was the only doctor and the only owner.

I am going to request the Honorable Federal Court may grant me compensatory relief for my business minimum $1,500,000.00 US$ Dollar.

52 – As of today 04/18/2017, since 12/01/2015, I have been not working. My License has been suspended. The average of the Nation basic salary for a Board Certified Internist, who has 30-years' experience, is much more than $250,000.00 a year. Salary from 12/01/2015 to 04/20/2017, {one year and five months} is US$350,000.00. {Exhibit no. M is my 2016 Fed. Tax Return}

I will request the Honorable Federal Court may grant me compensatory relief for my loss of work income, minimum US$350,000.00 US$ Dollar, plus I keep my rights to ask for relief from any pending loss from keeping my license suspended.

53 – I have been in my home in the state of strange kind of hostage, suffering from the severe stress of feeling injustice, humiliation, and

financial need. As a result of this stress, during April 2016, I was admitted twice in 2 hospitals {Garden City and Henry Ford Hospitals}, for Acute Coronary Syndrome, to rule out Heart Attack. The order damaged my reputation before my family, friends, my patients, hospitals, pharmacies' employees, public, and anybody who knows me, and the society. I have been suffering from the feeling of the stigma of being a bad person. I will request the Honorable Federal Court may grant me compensatory relief for the non-economic damage US$670,000.00.

54 - The requested total compensation relief is US$2,520,000.00 US Dollars plus $3,000,000., punitive relief and reinstatement of my medical license immediately.

VIII – Requested Reliefs

55 – I pray this Honorable Court may grant me the following reliefs against defendants: No: 1, Bill Schuette, No: 2, Dennis Szymanski, M.D., No: 3, Robert Regan, No:4, Andrew Hudson, No: 5, Jessica Taub, and No: 6, John Hopper, M.D. In their Individual capacity. This Court is authorized by 28 U.S.C.1331, 28 U.S.C.2201, and 28 U.S.C.2202, and MCL 691.1407(2) (c) and MCL 24.306, to grant these reliefs;

A – Declaratory relief, the Court may declare that my License was suspended minimum Six months and one day and $20,000 fine, order entered on 10/30/2015 was executed by the Board of Medicine, Disciplinary Subcommittee, without due process of Law in violations of US Constitution Amendment no: XIV.

B – Compensatory relief US$1,500,000.00 for destroying my Business (Astoria Medical P. C.) medical practice at 4811 Venoy Rd,

Wayne MI 48184, due to the suspension of my License. (Federal Tax Returns for four years Exhibit no. J).

C – Compensatory Relief for loss of work income from 12/1/2015 to 4/20/2017, one year and five months US$350,000.00 (My individual F. Tax Return Exhibit no. M).

D – Compensatory relief for non-economic damage US$670,000.00

E – Punitive relief US$ 3,000,000.00

F – Right for prospective compensatory relief from loss of work income

56 – I pray this Honorable Court may grant me the following reliefs against defendants, No: 7, Peter Graham, M.D. Chairperson of the Board of Medicine and

No: 8, Kim Gaedeke, director of Bureau of Professional Licensing. In their Official Capacity;

A – Prospective injunctive relief, reinstate my License to practice medicine immediately, By 28 U.S.C. 2201 and 28 U.S.C. 2202.

B – Right for prospective compensatory relief from loss of work income due to delay in the reinstatement of my License, By 28 U.S.C. 2202 and 28 U.S.C. 2202.

57 – Any further reliefs or orders, this Court may see them properly.

Respectfully Submitted

____________________________ April 18th 2017

Abdelbaset A Youssef, Pro Se, Plaintiff

CHAPTER 23

Detroit Federal Court Judge's Order

◆ ◆ ◆

THE FEDERAL COURT HAD DISMISSED my complaint about three reasons;

A - The subject of the complaint is state interest, and it is pending in state courts where I could raise constitutional questions,

B - Rocker-Feldman doctrine, which stands for the lower Federal Courts should not review the state court orders, and

C - Absolute Quasi-judicial Immunity shielded the defendants.

The Honorable Judge Robert's order

ORDER GRANTING DEFENDANTS' MOTION TO DISMISS

INTRODUCTION and BACKGROUND

On September 18, 2014, the Michigan Board of Medicine ("Board"), through its Disciplinary Committee, filed a complaint against Abdelbaset Abdelmagid Youssef ("Youssef") for prescribing 25,475 controlled substances between August 1, 2012, and July 31, 2013. Youssef was presented with a settlement offer. He rejected it and attended a disciplinary hearing instead. At the hearing, the Administrative Law Judge ("ALJ") issued a Proposal - adopted by the Board - that Youssef's license is suspended. Youssef applied for reinstatement; the Board denied the request.

Youssef exhausted appeals in the state court system and has an appeal pending in the Michigan Supreme Court. Youssef filed suit in the Eastern District of Michigan against Bill Schuette, Dennis Szymanski, Robert Regan, Andrew Hudson, Jessica Taub, Peter Graham, Kim Gaedeke (collectively "Defendants"). He asks the Court for redress not afforded to him through state court litigation.

Defendants move to dismiss under Fed. R. Civ. P. 12(b) (6).

Among other arguments,
Defendants say Youssef's claims are barred by the *Rooker-Feldman* doctrine, *Younger* abstention, absolute immunity and Eleventh Amendment immunity. The Court addresses each of these but finds the *Rooker-Feldman* doctrine is dispositive of all claims.

The Court **GRANTS** Defendants' motion.

Legal Standard

A complaint need not contain detailed factual allegations to survive a 12 (b)(6) motion. *Bell Atlantic Corp. v Twombly,* 550 U.S. 544, 555 (2007) (citing *Sanjuan v. American Bd. of Psychiatry and Neurology, Inc.,* 40 F.3d 247, 251 (C.A. 1994)). Fed. R. Civ. P. 8(a) requires a complaint to set forth "a short and plain statement of the claim showing that the pleader is entitled to relief," as well as a "demand for the relief sought." Fed. R. Civ. P. 8(a) (2), (3). The purpose of this rule is to give defendant fair notice of what is set forth in the plaintiff's claim and "the grounds upon which it rests." *Twombly,* 550 U.S. at 555 (quoting *Conley v. Gibson,* 355 U.S. 41,47 (1957). "Notice" pleading does not require detailed factual allegations but does require more than a bare assertion of legal conclusions. *Id.* A complaint "does not suffice if it tenders 'naked assertion[s]' devoid of 'further factual enhancement.' " *Ashcroft v. Iqbal,* 556 U.S. 662, 678 (2009) (quoting *Twombly,* 550 U.S. at 557).

Analysis

Role of Defendants

It is helpful to outline the role these Defendants played in the underlying state proceedings:

Andrew Hudson ("Hudson"), Assistant Attorney General, served as Attorney for the Board and filed a complaint against Youssef. Youssef says Hudson abused his authority as attorney for the Board because he did not respond to a motion Youssef filed;

Jessica Taub ("Taub"), Assistant Attorney General, served as Attorney for the Board. Youssef alleges Taub conspired with Hudson and the Administrative Law Judge ("ALJ");

Robert Regan ("Regan") works for the Michigan Department of Licensing and Regulatory Affairs. He conducted an investigation of Youssef's practice. Youssef accuses Regan of perjury and infringement. He does not say what Regan infringed;

Dennis Szymanski ("Szymanski") is a member of the Board. Youssef says Szymanski presented a final order for a vote without reviewing Youssef's exceptions to the ALJ's Proposal;

Bill Schuette ("Schuette") is Attorney General for the State of Michigan. He had no personal involvement in Youssef's state case. Youssef alleges that Schuette failed to comply with Youssef's request to remove Hudson from his licensing hearing. Youssef says Schuette's failure to remove Hudson was gross negligence and obstruction of justice;

Peter Graham ("Graham") is the Chairperson of Michigan Board of Medicine;

Kim Gaedeke ("Gaedeke") was a Director for the Bureau of Professional Licensing;

Dr. John Hopper ("Hopper") is referred to as an expert witness by Youssef. Youssef says he committed perjury at the hearing;

Adam Sadowski ("Sadowski") is an Assistant Attorney General; and Mark Donnelly ("Donnelly") is an Assistant Attorney General.

The *Rooker-Feldman* Doctrine Bars Youssef's Claims

The *Rooker-Feldman* doctrine bars a claim when "a plaintiff complains of injury from the state court judgment itself." *Coles v. Granville,* 448 F.3d 853, 858 (6th Cir. 2006). When the source of the injury claimed is a state court decision, the *Rooker-Feldman* doctrine prevents the district court from asserting jurisdiction and the court must dismiss the claim, *Steel Co. v. Citizens for a Better Env't,* 523 U.S. 83, 94 (1998).

Youssef complains that the state court orders are unsound; he asks the Court to overrule them. This is the very type of appellate review which the *Rooker-Feldman* doctrine bars. All of his claims are precluded.

Any Claims that May Arise on Appeal are barred by *Younger* Abstention. Defendants argue any claims that may arise on appeal are barred by *Younger* abstention. There are three requirements that must be met for *Younger* abstention to apply: "(1) there must be ongoing state judicial proceedings; (2) those proceedings must implicate important state interests; and (3) there must be an adequate opportunity in the state proceedings to raise constitutional challenges." *Squire v. Coughlan,* 469 F.3d 551, 555 (6th Cir. 2006) (quoting *Sun Ref. & Mktg. Co. v. Brennan,* 921 F.2d 635, 639 (6th Cir. 1990). *Squire* noted that federal courts should abstain unless there is an extraordinary circumstance that would make abstention inappropriate, *Squire,* 469 F.2d at 555.

Here, the three factors are satisfied. First, there are an "ongoing state judicial proceedings;" Youssef appealed the suspension of his license to the Michigan Supreme Court; that appeal is pending, and he sues on the same injury here.

Second, the state has an important interest to ensure that doctors appropriately prescribe controlled substances. The Court considers Youssef's inappropriate conduct as contrary to the public's best interest. The second element is satisfied.

Finally, Youssef had ample opportunity in state proceedings to raise constitutional challenges. He opted for a hearing, employed a lawyer to represent him, "retired" that lawyer, pled his case in front of the district and appeals court, and filed an appeal in the Michigan Supreme Court.

The *Younger* abstention requirements are met. To the extent there may be any disagreement that the *Rooker-Feldman* doctrine is dispositive on all issues, Youssef's claims are barred by *Younger* abstention.

Absolute Immunity Bars Youssef's claims against Defendants

Absolute immunity "is necessary to assure that judges, advocates, and witnesses can perform their respective functions without harassment or intimidation." *Butz v. Economou,* 438 U.S. 478, 512 (1978). The court extends absolute immunity beyond judicial officials' to prosecutors and parties participating in the judicial process so that they enjoy the same protections. *Id.* The roles of Taub, Hudson, Regan, Schuette, and Hopper are described above. They were all part of the judicial process in state court and are entitled to absolute immunity.

The holding in *Butz* extends to members of medical boards and affords Szymanski absolute immunity as well. In *Quatkemeyer, a* doctor was investigated for excessively prescribing controlled substances; his license was revoked. *Quatkemeyer v. Kentucky Bd. of Med. Licensure,* 506 F. App'x 342, 343 (6th Cir. 2012). The doctor brought suit against the Kentucky Board of Medical Licensure, challenging its determination that he should be denied access to controlled substances. The Kentucky Board moved to dismiss, and the district court granted the motion. On appeal, the Sixth Circuit affirmed and found that the board was entitled to absolute immunity. The same result is required here. Because Szymanski is a member of the Board, he is afforded absolute immunity.

All Defendants are entitled to Eleventh Amendment Immunity

Defendants argue they are entitled to Eleventh Amendment Immunity. The Court agrees. The Eleventh Amendment affords states immunity from suits commenced or prosecuted ... by citizens of another state." U.S. Const., Amend. XI., The Supreme Court extends immunity to those sued in their official capacity. *Will v. Michigan Dep't of State Police,* 491 U.S. 58, 59 (1989). "A suit against state officials in their official capacities is not a suit against the officials but rather is a suit against the officials' offices and, thus, is no different from a suit against the state itself." *Id.*

Because claims are brought against all of the Defendants in their official capacities, all are entitled to Eleventh Amendment Immunity.

Youssef's claims against Graham and Gaedeke Fail Youssef lists Graham and Gaedeke, in their official capacity, in the caption of the complaint. He also lists Sadowski and Donnelly in the caption. He fails to make any allegations against these four individuals. The Court dismissed them. *See Frazier v. Michigan,* 41 F. App'x 762, 764 (6th Cir. 2002) (dismissing claims where complaint did not allege which of the named defendants was personally involved in or responsible for each alleged violation of rights).

Conclusion

Youssef's claims are dismissed in their entirety. The Court need not address qualified or *respondent superior* liability, also raised by Youssef.

The Court GRANTS Defendants' Motion to Dismiss.

Youssef has the following motions pending:

Motion for Preliminary Injunction [Doc. #25];

Motion to Amend Motion for Preliminary Injunction [Doc. #33];

Motion for Order to Start Discovery [Doc. #36]; and

Motion for Leave to File Supplemental Brief [Doc. #37].

By this Order dismissing his case, the motions are deemed **MOOT**.

IT IS ORDERED.

S/Victoria A. Roberts

Victoria A. Roberts United States District Judge

Dated: August 10, 2017, the undersigned certifies that a copy of this document was served on the attorneys of record by electronic means or U.S. Mail on August 10, 2017.

s/Linda Vertriest

Deputy Clerk

CHAPTER 24

Complaint in the Michigan Court of Claims

◆ ◆ ◆

THE FEDERAL COURT HAD DISMISSED my complaint about the subject of the complaint is state interest, and it is pending in state courts where I could raise constitutional questions. Even though the complaint was dismissed in the Federal Court for lack of jurisdiction, I had a chance to file the same complaint in the Michigan Court of Claims.

THE STATE OF MICHIGAN
MICHIGAN COURT OF CLAIMS

925 W. Ottawa
Lansing, Michigan, 48933
Docket No. 17-000229-MM Honorable: Michael Talbot

Complaint about Constitutional Questions
For Declaratory, Injunctive, Compensatory and punitive reliefs
Abdelbaset Abdelmagid Youssef

Plaintiff

Vs.

1 – Department of Licensing and Regulatory Affairs (LARA)
2 – Bureau of Professional Licensing
3 – Board of Medicine

4 – Dennis Szymanski, M.D., member of the Board of Medicine.
5 – Robert Regan, R. Ph. Investigator, at LARA
6 – Andrew Hudson, Assistant Attorney General.
7 – Jessica Taub, Assistant Attorney General.
8– John Hopper M.D. Expert witness, work for LARA.

Defendants

I - Statement of Jurisdiction

This Court has original jurisdiction on the matter by US Constitution: Article XIV Amendment 14), ("nor shall any State deprive any person of life, liberty, or property, without due process of law; nor deny to any person within its jurisdiction the equal protection of the laws," and

Michigan Constitution Article I: "Sec.17. No person shall be compelled in any criminal case to be a witness against himself, nor be deprived of life, liberty or property, without due process of law. The right of all individuals, firms, corporations and voluntary associations to fair and just treatment in the course of legislative and executive investigations and hearings shall not be infringed.

Through MCL 600.6419, MCL 691.1407, MCL 24.304, MCL 24.306 and the other relevant Laws and Statues.

II - The Statements of Facts

A - Gross Negligence: Defective Complaint

1 – On 9/18/2014, Mr. Hudson, AAG, filed the complaint. Since it was in pain management, I did not expect the writer did not know the basics of medicine. Nothing in the complaint has any legal value. The writer, through the complaint, was writing about Tylenol as the controlled medicine. There is nothing else relevant to the complaint. When I filed an answer, I claimed that the writer was doing fraud. Only

after seven months, on 4/23/2015, during the hearing, I had known that the writer was Mr. Hudson. We entered into a personal conflict. He stated that he did that because the subject is outside his experiences. MCL 333.16228 requires the Board of Medicine that the complaint in controlled medicine should be reviewed by a controlled prescription panel of 10 physicians before filing. The Board of Medicine does not have a nurse to review it.

B - Infringed Hearing

2 – On November 2014, I was investigated by Rosalie Tocco Bradley, M.D., Ph.D. consultant of pain management and member of the Board of Medicine. In the presence of Mr. Hudson, she stated that I was seeing very sick people and I was doing well.

3 – On 11/4/2014, Mr. Hudson had sent to me offer for settlement, among its conditions I had to pay $5000 fine. I refused to pay if they did not say what wrong I did. I requested hearing to get relief. I practiced my legal rights.

4 – Mr. Hudson selected ALJ related to the victim. On 4/23/2015, during the hearing, the ALJ told Mr. Hudson, he noticed one of the witnesses was his cousin. Mr. Hudson said: yes Judge, she is and he added; she is the complainant for her son, B.S. as well.

5 – Robert Regan, R. Ph. Works for LARA, Defendant no. 5.

A – During the hearing, on 4/23/2015, he testified clear lies outside the scope of the allegations of the complaint to mislead the ALJ.

B – (PFD, finding facts no. 7 – 11). He stated: because of respondent's patients in the market of diversion, they have to go far to get the pharmacy that dispenses their prescriptions, so they aggregate in pharmacies mostly far away, at Bellavista, Pharmor, Friendly, and Knight Drug Pharmacies.

The first Pharmacy was cross street from my office at 388 Inkster Rd, Inkster MI 48141. The second one was inside my office. When he came, he asked me how much rent I was collecting from it. The third one is close to my office so that he saw its flyers in the waiting room and asked me to stop that.

C – He said that I prescribe Hydrocodone, while Dr. Honet (Pain consultant) prescribes Morphine, while he knew at that time Hydrocodone was DEA schedule III and Morphine was II. We were allowed to give five refills for Schedule III, in one visit, but no refill for Morphine. He tried to make the ALJ thinks Morphine is safer than Hydrocodone, as I was giving Hydrocodone to the ALJ's relative.

6 - John Hopper, M.D., Works for LARA and its expert witness, Defendant no. 8.

A – He was the expert witness in the hearing, on 4/23/2015. He was spraying lies without any restrictions. He testified lies not only in the subjects related to the complaint but also subjects not related to the complaint. He filed report included three unknown patients. The report contains lies as well.

B – He was not qualified to testify as expert witness in chronic pain management case, as he has never treated a single case of pain management in primary care.

C – I filed three motions to exempt him from being an expert witness and exempt his testimony and his report. My motions were denied for unknown reasons.

D – Examples of his lies; respondent was giving B.S. (ALJ's relative) 10 mg Hydrocodone, then 10 mg Hydrocodone is equal to 750 mg

Morphine. Any textbook from Tokyo to New York says 10 mg Hydrocodone equal to 10 mg oral Morphine or 3.3 mg injectable Morphine. Another lie, the maximum dose of Xanax is 1 mg, while there are tablets of Xanax 3 mg. The maximum daily dose is 10 mg, could be more in case of emergency. (PFD fact: 15-20). Most of his testimonies were lies and outside the scope of the complaint.

7 – The witnesses directed their grave lies about patient B.S, the ALJ's relative. They drew scenario as if I almost kill him. To make the ALJ loses his impartiality.

8 – Many lie in the PFD, I answered them in my Exceptions to the PFD. I supported my answers in Exceptions with copies from 3 standard textbooks. Even I shipped the three textbooks to Mr. Hudson. I answered each fact and each conclusion of Law with undisputable evidence. Mr. Hudson has never disputed any of my evidence.

C - Order in Violation of Law

8 – Even though, I had known that: Mr. Hudson conspired with Mr. Regan and Dr. Hopper to fabricate infringed hearing, I felt that there was hope to be corrected in the Board of Medicine, Disciplinary subcommittee.

Law, R 792.10131, they have to review my exceptions before the order became final, *R 792.10131 (3) A decision shall become a final decision in the absence of exceptions or review by an entity with final decision authority and*

MCL 333.16237(3) In reviewing the recommended findings of fact and conclusions of law of the hearings examiner and the record of the hearing, a disciplinary subcommittee may request the hearings examiner to take additional testimony or evidence on a specific issue or may revise the recommended findings of fact and conclusions of law as determined necessary by the disciplinary subcommittee, or both.

9 – I was shocked by defendant no: 4, Dennis Szymanski, M.D., member of the Board of Medicine. He presented the final order for voting on the Board, without reviewing my exceptions to the PFD as described by law. Even he did not mention them.

11 – Discovery is required to know if Dr. Szymanski had intentionally ignored my Exceptions to the PFD or Mr. Hudson had never presented my Exceptions to the committee as a part of his retaliation plot.

C – The relevant allegations are: 19, 20, 24, 25, 32, 33, 35, 37, 39, and 40. All of them are summarized by the Allegation no. 16 items {a thru f}. Because the ALJ did not rule on items d thru f and dismissed them; I have to address only the items {a thru c}.

12 - The next is quoted from my exceptions to PFD, a previous chapter in this book.

A – Allegation 16 (a) Failure to consider the use of other treatment modalities or non-narcotic pain medications. Every patient in my office including these four patients has, at least, one non-narcotic pain medicine in each visit. Regarding other modalities, the main subject of discussion during the visit every visit for each patient is considering other modalities. No one in this four patient; candidate for other modality, patient B.S. left my office since 2012; his mother testified that he has never received physical therapy or other modality for pain. In my exceptions I asked the Petitioner may assign one patient, who needed other modality but I deprived him. I presented copies from the standard textbook of pain management, show that I was doing the same as the books and I asked the Petitioner to bring any textbook says otherwise.

B – Allegation 16(b), Failure to consistently monitor for abuse and diversion by urine drug test or MAPS. For the last ten years, I see only patients who have chronic pain. No doctor could work in pain management without monitoring for abuse or diversion. PFD finding fact # 13 states that I was monitoring MAPS. If I do not monitor, how the four patients MAPS are clean? Patient B.S. had few times small amounts of controlled medicine from the ER. The pain contract, that every patient I have authorized him/her to get help from the E.R. The Petitioner's expert witness agreed that shortage of pain medicine could put the patient in the risk of death (Transcript p.116 lines 10-17). Patient K.B. had duplicated three prescriptions in 2011 because she did not know Ativan and Xanax belong to the same family of medicine.

I check the MAPS every visit, but I do not print it if it is O.K. as there is no need for counseling. No guideline or Statue or recommendation mandates printing the MAPS or Urine Drug test result even if it is OK.

C – Allegation 16 (c) prescribing an inappropriate combination of medication. In any textbook; standard treatment for chronic back pain syndrome secondary to structural damage in the spinal cord is pain medicine + Muscle relaxant + Antianxiety, Narcotics and Soma and Xanax all are approved by the FDA either in combination or separate. Xanax is approved as the first line of treatment for pain-related anxiety. In my Exceptions, I discussed that and presented copies of textbooks to support my statement and asked the petitioner to present any textbook states otherwise.

D - Obstruction of Justice

13 – On 11/13/2015, I filed a claim of Appeal and motion for a stay order. The Court of Appeals denied staying because *MCR 7.209(2)*

motion for bond or a stay pending appeal may not be filed in the Court of Appeals unless such a motion was decided by the trial court.

14 – On 11/25/2015, I filed a motion to stay on the Board of Medicine. Mr. Hudson, who was in charge of the case as an attorney to the Board has never answered the motion in violation of MCL24.304, to deprive the Court of Appeals Jurisdiction on the matter of stay in a typical case of obstruction of Justice.

15 – On 2/11/2016, I filed complaint to Mr. Hudson's supervisor, (Mr. Bill Schuette, the State Attorney General), that Mr. Andrew Hudson, Assistant Attorney General, has been conspiring with Mr. Ronald Regan R. Ph., and Hopper M.D., to subject me to severe cycles of torture as retaliation for a personal conflict, requesting to investigate the situation or keep them away from my business to save me from deadly stress.

I requested if he may investigate the situation to relieve me from deadly stress as I was admitted twice in 2 hospitals for cardiac issues related to this kind of strange stress or he may change him by another AAG. Mr. Schuette has never answered my complaints.

E - Infringed Hearing second time

16 – After I lost hope for staying pending appeals, on 3/5/2016, I applied for reinstatement. Just one day before the end of the six months suspension, Mr. Hudson had resumed his retaliation. He filed a frivolous opposition.

17 – On 7/5/2016, during a hearing for reinstatement of the License, Mr. Hudson conspired with defendant no: 7, Jessica Taub, AAG, to infringe the hearing.

A – During the hearing, on 7/5/2016, she told the ALJ, that I am not eligible for reinstatement because since I have filed Appeal, I still do not admit my mistakes. I answered under oath that I filed an appeal because the witnesses committed perjury.

B – On 7/5/2016, during the Hearing for reinstatement of my License before ALJ Plummer, she presented a fabricated document and witness who told lies under oath. She did this fraud to prove that I was not honest so that I would not be eligible for reinstatement.

F - Obstruction of Justice second time

18 – I filed a motion to open the record and remove this document, as I presented evidence that it is false, but the ALJ, after she failed to answer the motion, returned it for the record was closed in violation of: *{R 792.10115 Motion practice. (2) All motions shall be filed at least 14 days prior to the date set for hearing unless other scheduling provisions prevent compliance with this timeline or the need for the motion could not reasonably have been foreseen 14 days prior to the hearing.*

19 – My attorney's business is specialized in physicians' licenses, so his business is through them. She sent email to my attorney practicing pressure on him to make him force me to withdraw the motion, *so I retired him.*

G - Order in illegal retaliation

20 – In PFD for reinstatement of my license, The ALJ said in the PFD finding facts 11 thru 14, Due to the short period of suspension, he still claims that he was tricked by the Authorities when he committed an act of incompetence, etc. ALJ recommended denying until I understand, as he stated.

21 – On 9/28/2016, I filed another complaint with Mr. Bill Schuette, State Attorney General. I stated: I, Abdelbaset A Youssef, M.D., hereby raise to your honor this complaint. Because of a personal conflict with

Andrew Hudson, Assistant Attorney General, he and Jessica Taub Assistant Attorney general have conspired with the Administrative Law Judge Peter Plummer to commit a grave crime against me. They illegally delayed deciding reinstatement of my license, and they are going to deny it. They use hunger, to defend my Appeal that I filed on 11/13/2015, against their order on 10/30/2015, suspending my License, instead of using the legal way. Mr. Bill Schuette, State Attorney General, again ignored my complaint.

22 – On 1/31/2017, I filed a supplemental brief in the Court of Appeals may consider the new order denying reinstatement along with the original order of suspension six months subject to the Appeal.

23 – The Court of Appeals has returned the brief as it had not had Jurisdiction over the new order. I have to appeal the new order in the Circuit Court. If the Circuit reversed the order, the Board of Medicine has a chance to appeal the Circuit Court's reverse to the Court of Appeals. The new season will take at least two more years.

24 – Suspension was for six months, while the appeal to get relief from it, without a stay, takes 18 months, even still I have to go to another Court. I need more than three years, without work, to get relief from 6 months suspension.

III - Conclusion

Count 1, Gross Negligence

25 – Mr. Hudson wrote a defective complaint in a subject outside his experience that resulted in the personal conflict. MCL 333.16228, states that even regular physician cannot write a complaint in Controlled medicine, so the Statue required that the controlled prescriptions panel should review this kind of complaints. A reasonable

official in the position of Mr. Hudson would not write a complaint in medicine when it was outside his experience, or he does not know the basics of medicine. It is clear; that his act is gross negligence planted seeds for the damages.

Count 2, infringed hearing

26 – Mr. Hudson selected the ALJ conducting the hearing, who is the cousin of the complainant, mother of Patient B.S. The reasonable official in his position knows the selection of ALJ's cousin of the complainant is illegal as it was for infringing the hearing in violation of the Constitutions

27 – Mr. Hudson lied and conspired with Defendant no: 5, Mr. Regan and no: 8, Dr. Hopper to commit grave lies about management of B.S., ALJ's relative. If he did not know that they were testifying lies, I filed to him my Exceptions to PFD stated with evidence that they testified lies, among this evidence three standard textbooks. A reasonable official in his position knows, even if he is not a physician, from these evidence that witnesses were testifying lies under oath.

Count 3, perjury under oath

28 – Discovery will give me a chance to get further proofs that Mr. Regan had testified lies under oath in conspiracy with Mr. Hudson. I will prove that he committed grave lies. The reasonable pharmacist knows that a pharmacy inside the same building with a medical office, cross the street from it, or 1.24 mile from it is not considered far away from that office. The reasonable pharmacist knows that narcotic DEA schedule II is not safer than schedule III. Schedule III is safer than schedule II, so we can give the patient up to 6 month supply in refills in one

visit. We cannot give any refill for Schedule II. He did that along with many other lies in the hearing transcript to attack the ALJ's impartiality, as he was testifying lies about management of ALJ's cousin's son.

29 – Dr. Hopper had been spraying lies under oath without restrictions. Any reasonable Physician or Physician Assistant knows 10 mg Hydrocodone equal to 10 mg Morphine, not 750 mg or he knows the maximum dose of Xanax is not 1 mg, as there is tablet 3 mg Xanax. He told this lies to make the ALJ thinks as if I almost kill his cousin's son. Discovery will help me prove many more lies.

Count 4: order in violation of Laws

30 – Discovery by testimony, will give me a chance to know if defendant no: 4, Dr. Szymanski intentionally violated the Laws when he presented the order for voting without reviewing my Exceptions to the PFD or Mr. Hudson had never delivered the Exceptions to the Board of Medicine, as a part of his plot.

Without Discovery I cannot know whether Dr. Szymanski or Mr. Hudson responsible for violation of the Laws R 792.10131 and MCL 333.16237.

Count 5, Obstruction of Justice

31 – After I filed a claim of Appeal, on 11/25/2015, I filed a motion to stay order on the Board of Medicine, as Mr. Hudson was in charge to be an attorney for the Board. I mailed him the original of the motion. He has never answered the motion neither denies nor grants or said anything. Reasonable official knows no answer is a violation of MCL 24.304(1). No answer, due to MCR 7.209, deprive the Court of Appeals Jurisdiction on the matter. He knows this act causes a great

deal of damage and if the Court of appeals vacates the order after 18 months, its order will be valueless. Reasonable official knows that this act is intentional infliction of damage.

32 – On 2/11/2016, I filed a complaint with Mr. Bill Schuette, State Attorney General, that Mr. Hudson, due to the personal conflict was targeting me, causing deadly stress. I mailed a copy to Mr. Hudson as well. The ethics require Mr. Hudson either recuse himself or states why he did not recuse himself.

Count 6; Infringed hearing second time

33 – On 7/5/2016, Mr. Hudson conspired with defendant no: 7, Jessica Taub, AAG, during a hearing for reinstating of my license, she presented false document and illegal statements to issue a new order extended the suspension of my license to be minimum two years. She practiced pressure on my Attorney to force me to withdraw the motion to remove false document after she failed to answer it.

VI - Damages subject of the requested reliefs

34 – The defendants, illegal acts had destroyed my medical practice, the business that my family and I had built, over 13 years. The business was Solo primary care medical practice, Internal Medicine/pain management, {Astoria Medical P C) at 4811 Venoy Rd. Wayne, Michigan 48184. Upon closing the practice, it had about six thousand files and 878 active patients, and I was the only doctor in it and the only owner of it. On 12/01/2015, to be compliant with the order, I stopped working and informed the patients that my License was suspended to find another office. If my License were reinstated, I need at least 13 years to build one like it.

35 - I am going to request the Honorable Court of Claims may grant me compensatory relief for my business minimum US$1,500,000.00.

36 – Since12/01/2015, I have been not working. My License has been suspended. The average of the Nation basic salary for a Board Certified Internist, who has 30-year experience, is much more than US$250,000.00 a year.

37 – I have been in my home in the state of strange kind of hostage, suffering from the severe stress of feeling injustice, humiliation, and financial need. As a result of this stress, during April 2016, I was admitted twice in 2 hospitals {Garden City and Henry Ford Hospitals). The Order damaged my reputation before my family, friends, my patients, hospitals, pharmacies' employees, public, and anybody who knows me, and the society.

IV – Requested Reliefs

38 – I pray the honorable Michigan Court of Claims may grant me order against all defendants jointly or severely and on their official and individual capacities:

A – Declaratory relief; the Court may declare that my License was suspended minimum six months and one day, and $20,000 fine, order entered on 10/30/2015. The suspension was extended by the order denying reinstatement entered on 12/21/2016. It was executed without due process of Law.

B - Injunction of retaliation by the reinstatement of my medical License immediately.

39 – I pray the Honorable Michigan Court of Claims may grant me the following reliefs, jointly or severally, against defendants; No: 4, Dennis Szymanski, M.D., No: 5, Robert Regan, No:6, Andrew

Hudson, No: 7, Jessica Taub, and No: 8, John Hopper, M.D, In their Individual capacities:

A – Compensatory relief, minimum $1,500,000.00 for destroying my Business,

B – Compensatory Relief for loss of work income from 12/1/2015 to the date of reinstatement, minimum $250,000.00 a year.

C–Compensatory relief for non-economic damage, US$670,000.00

E – Punitive relief US$ 3,000,000.00. F – Attorney Fee.

40 – Any further reliefs or orders, this Court may see them properly.

I testify under penalty of perjury that all statements are true as best knowledge

Respectfully Submitted

____________________________ August 15th 2017

Abdelbaset A Youssef, Pro Se, Plaintiff

CHAPTER 25

Request the Court may enjoin violations

◆ ◆ ◆

After I filed the complaint in the Court of Claims, I filed this motion for preliminary injunction. The legal proceeding takes years, so it is difficult to stay without work for years. I was authorized by law to file a motion for preliminary reinstatement of my medical license while the case was still pending to decrease the damages.

THE STATE OF MICHIGAN
MICHIGAN COURT OF CLAIMS

925 W. Ottawa St

P. O. Box 30185, Lansing, MI, 48909

Docket No. 17-000229-MM Honorable: Michael Talbot

Abdelbaset A Youssef, MD

Plaintiff

Vs.

1. Department of Licensing and Regulatory Affairs, et al

Defendants

BRIEF IN SUPPORT OF PLAINTIFF'S MOTION FOR PRELIMINARY INJUNCTION

I, Abdelbaset A Youssef, the Pro Se plaintiff, hereby certify under penalty of perjury that the following statements, affidavits, and exhibits are true, as my best knowledge.

Statement of Facts

1– On 10/30/2015, the Board of Medicine had entered order suspended my License minimum six months and one day. By Law, I could apply for reinstatement within 90 days before the end of the suspension. These 90 days are for processing the application so that the License may be reinstated timely.

2 - On 3/5/2016, I filled application for reinstatement. On 2/12/2017, I received decision denying my application. It took more than 11 months to review the application. This delay in deciding the application is not only an intentional violation of due process of Law, but it is amazing kind of torture and inflicting damage.

3 - Just one day before the License should be reinstated, defendant no: 6, Andrew Hudson, AAG, filed frivolous opposition stating I was not honest.

4 – During the hearing, while I was testifying under oath, in cross-examination, defendant no: 7, Jessica Taub, AAG, stated that: since I have appealed the original order, I do not admit my mistakes, so I was not eligible for reinstatement. I answered that I filed an appeal because the hearing for the original order was infringed and the witnesses committed grave perjury under oath.

5 - She asked me to read a sentence in my affidavit, {*my plan to restart my practice*}. This affidavit was submitted with my application for reinstatement. This sentence is on page 1, paragraph B, line 5, *(I have stopped prescribing a combination of Narcotic, Soma, and Xanax, since 2012, I*

told Mr. Regan, R. Ph. (investigator), in 2013, that I have stopped prescribing this combination, except for few patients, it is risky to stop it).

6 – The AAG asked me, how much is the few, I stated: from 20 to 30. She presented three exhibits, C. D, and E, stating that I gave this trinity, at least one time, during 2013, to 493 patients, during 2014, to 334 patients, and during 2015, to 33 patients. She claimed that she get this information from the MAPS, which is an official source. She considered me lied.

6 – The matter is not about giving this trinity but they claimed that I lied, when I stated in the affidavit that: in 2013: {*that I have stopped prescribing etc., except for few it is risky to stop it*}. I supposed to state: *I have **gradually** stopped* prescribing ... except for few, because I gave the Trinity to 334 patients during 2014, so I am in lack good moral character for committing lie.

7 – Standard treatment regime for back pain due to herniated spinal disc is Narcotic pain medicine, Xanax for pain related Anxiety and Soma for Muscle spasm. In 2012, DEA regulated Soma to be controlled medicine. One pharmacist told me that the State Pharmacist does not like to see this trinity too often. To please the State Pharmacist, I started to change the trinity to replace Soma by another noncontrolled muscle relaxant. In 2013, I told Mr. Regan that I was trying gradually to replace Soma with another muscle relaxant. No one told me to do that, and this trinity is still FDA approved for treating these conditions. Patient, who is stable on this regime for years, it was not easy, and it could be risky to change this regime. I started to change in 2013, by the end of 2014 through 2015; I succeeded to change except for few patients it was risky to change it for them.

8 – In my Affidavit *(my plan to restart my practice),* I started this sentence that I have stopped prescribing except for few. I did not write

this Affidavit in 2013, I wrote it in 2016. The conclusion is that: I have stopped gradually, by closing my practice (during 2015), only a few patients had received this trinity at least one time. I had gone down from 493 in 2013 to 33, at the end of 2014. 33 is few in relation to 493. I did not lie in my testimony when I stated that the few are from 20 to 30. {*I have stopped prescribing except for few*}.

9 – I do not need to lie. I am not required to write this sentence in my affidavit at all, or I could just add word gradually. I am not required to do not give this trinity if it is indicated. There is no DEA, FDA or any federal or state regulation or any research or scientific paper recommend do not give this trinity if it is indicated. All that I did was to please the State Pharmacist at the same time treat my patients right and safely to avoid undue hassle with the State Pharmacist.

10 – Because I do not have access to this official source, during the hearing, my attorney and I did not admit these Exhibits.

11 – After I went home, even I did not have access to their official source; I was able to review charts of six patients out of these 33 patients, in their Exhibit no. E. I discovered that: I have never given this trinity to these six patients, not only in 2015 but never in my office. So these exhibits contain forgery.

12 – My Attorney refused to file a motion to the ALJ may open the record and remove these exhibits for they contain forgery. I filed this motion on my own.

14 – My attorney tried to make me withdraw the motion. I refused to submit to his continuous pressure. He forwarded an email was sent to him from defendant no; 7, Jessica Taub, AAG, asked him to withdraw the motion. I felt, in the message, smell of pressure and deal. My attorney business is specialized in medical licenses, so I retired him for he could not help me.

15 – After Jessica Taub had failed to answer the motion by the deadline, the ALJ returned the motion for the record was closed in violation of: {*R 792.10115 Motion practice. (2) All motions shall be filed at least 14 days prior to the date set for hearing unless other scheduling provisions prevent compliance with this timeline or the need for the motion could not reasonably have been foreseen 14 days prior to hearing*}.

16 – On 9/21/2016, ALJ had filed the PFD. He stated all requirements for reinstatement were satisfied, but he recommended denying my application for only the next two items:

A – In reference to my appeal in the Court of Appeals about the original order suspended my License. *The ALJ stated in finding facts 10 – 13.* {*Due to a short period of suspension, he failed to come to a full understanding of his conduct and accept his responsibility and continue to claim that he was tricked by authorities when committed an act of incompetence*}. No dispute that this statement is illegal and it should not be stated by a Judge, and it violates the due process.

B – I am in lack of good moral character, the ALJ based his conclusion on the up mentioned exhibits, presented, during the hearing by defendant no: 7, Jessica Taub, AAG. These exhibits were not admitted, and during all of the stages of the proceeding, they failed to dispute that they contain forgery and even if they are true there is no dispute that they do not establish lack of good moral character.

17 – On 9/26/2016, I filed Exception to the PFD and re-filed the returned motion about the forgery in the exhibits to the Board of Medicine, as I am authorized to re-file it by {*R 792.10131(1)*}. The Board of Medicine has never answered it as well.

18 – On 9/28/28, I filed a complaint against the ALJ, Mr. Andrew Hudson, and Jessica Taub to the State Attorney General and

I forwarded a copy of the Complaint to the ALJ, and the defendants: no. 6, Andrew Hudson, no. 7, Jessica Taub, no. 3, chairperson of the Board of Medicine and no. 2, the director of Bureau of Professional Licensing. I had never received an answer.

19 – On Feb. 12th, 2017, I received the order denying reinstatement. The Board of Medicine issued the order without answering my motion and my exceptions to the PFD and in clear violation of:

MCL338.45, Finding person unqualified; statement; rehearing. Sec. 5.

When a person is found to be unqualified for a license because of a lack of good moral character, or similar criteria, the person shall be furnished by the board or agency with a statement to this effect. The statement shall contain a complete record of the evidence upon which the determination was based. The person shall be entitled, as of right, to a rehearing on the issue before the board if he or she has relevant evidence not previously considered, regarding his or her qualifications}.

Argument

I – Legal standard; In determining whether a party is entitled to a preliminary injunction, courts must consider the following four factors: (1) a substantial likelihood of success on the merits; (2) a substantial threat of irreparable injury; (3) whether the issuance of the injunction will cause substantial harm to others if issued; and (4) whether the public interest is served by issuance of the injunction, *Nightclub inc. v. The city of Paducab, 202 F.3d 884 (6th Cir.2000).* These factors are not prerequisites, but are factors that are to be balanced against each other," *U.S. v. Edward Rose & Sons, 384 F.3d 258, 261 (6th Cir. 2004).*

II – Likely I will succeed in the merit of denying reinstatement of the License which is issue independent of the other claims:

A - The original order is suspension the License minimum six months and one day and $20.000 fine. So far, the License has been suspended for 22 months, and the $20,000 fine was paid, on time.

B - There is no genuine dispute that all of the conditions of reinstatement described by State Law; *MCL 333.16245(6), are satisfied.*

MCL 333.16248: A registration; board may reinstate a registration revoked or suspended under this part if, after a hearing, the board is satisfied by clear and convincing evidence that the individual is of good moral character, has the education and experience as required in this article, has met the criteria in the rules promulgated under section 16245(6), in accordance with this article.

C - The ALJ's proposal for decision certified that all of the requirements for reinstatement, under MCL 333.16245(6), have been satisfied. The Board of Medicine adopted this PFD.

D –The ALJ had done mistake when he considered appealing the original order bars reinstatement. Practicing legal rights is not mentioned as a condition for reinstatement in MCL 333.16245(6).

E - I am in lack of good moral character, the ALJ based his conclusion on exhibits contains fabricated information. Defendants have not disputed, and they cannot dispute that these exhibits contain forgery.

F – If we considered the exhibits are true; in my Affidavit (my plan to restart my practice); I stated: that I have stopped prescribing except for few. So if I went down from 493 during 2013 to 33, by the end of 2014, I told the truth. 33 are few in relation to 493, I did not lie, and I did not need to lie. These exhibits do not indicate lack of good moral character, as described in MCL 338.41, 338.42, 338.43, and 338.45:

MCL 338.42 Judgment of guilt in criminal prosecution or judgment in a civil action as evidence in determining good moral character; consideration of a certificate of employability; rebuttal.

(1) A judgment of guilt in a criminal prosecution or judgment in a civil action shall not be used, in and of itself, by a licensing board or agency as proof of an individual's lack of good moral character. However, the licensing board or agency may use that judgment as evidence in the determination of his or her good moral character.

(2) If a judgment of guilt in a criminal prosecution is used as evidence in the determination of an individual's good moral character under subsection (1), the licensing board or agency shall also consider his or her certificate of employability, if any, under section 34d of the corrections code of 1953, 1953 PA 232, MCL 791.234d, as evidence in the determination.

(3) If a judgment of guilt in a criminal proceeding or a judgment in a civil action is used under subsection (1) as evidence of an individual's lack of good moral character, the licensing board or agency shall notify the individual and he or she is permitted to rebut the evidence by showing that at the current time he or she has the ability to, and is likely to, serve the public in a fair, honest, and open manner, that he or she is rehabilitated, or that the substance of the former offense is not reasonably related to the occupation or profession for which he or she is seeking a license.

G – On 3/5/2016, I filled application for reinstatement. On 2/12/2017, I received the decision to deny my application. It took more than 11 months to review the application. This is not only an intentional violation of due process of Law, but it is amazing kind of torture as well. Unreasonable delay of reviewing the application for reinstatement is a violation of due process & proves intentional infliction of damage.

III – Irreparable damage if the motion were not granted;

Since 12/1/2015, neither my wife nor I have been working. Since then, we do not have income. My sons, even doctors they are still residents, both have families; they are not able to help me. My home is in pending foreclosure due to no payment since December last year. Last year I sold my apartment in Florida and three cars. I have a history of Diabetes and heart disease; I am a survivor of heart attack and cardiac arrest. Due to this stress, last year, I was admitted twice to two hospitals. This stress of injustice, humiliation, and financial need threaten my life.

IV – Defendants do not dispute that: the application for reinstatement and the ALJ's proposal for decision had certified that I meet all requirements for reinstatement including the public interest and no harm to anybody if the license is reinstated. My experiences in pain management and my work in my offices in Inkster and Wayne cities, which are medically underserved areas and standing for enforcing the constitutions are further evidence for the public interest.

V – Defendants do not dispute that there is no harm if the License was reinstated. In the far beginning of the proceeding, on 11/4/2014 I was investigated by Rosalie Tocco Bradley, M. D., pain consultant and member of the Board of Medicine, who stated that it was OK to keep working. Mr. Hudson had offered me a settlement for $5,000 fine and kept working as well. I refused to pay the fine and requested hearing to get relief from paying the fine. This is evidence that they do not dispute that there is no harm if the License is reinstated.

VI – Accordingly; there is no genuine dispute that the order was issued without due process of Law in violation of the U. S. and State Constitutions and Statues. Reinstatement of my License has been due since May 31, 2016. I am entitled to reinstatement of my license according to the conditions of Michigan Statues.

Requested Relief

There is no genuine dispute that the application for reinstatement was denied through intentional violation of the due process of Law. The State official did forgery, gross negligence and intentional infliction of damages. I pray the honorable Court may grant me motion for preliminary injunction reinstate my License according to the State regulations and Statues immediately.

Respectfully Submitted

Abdelbaset A Youssef, September 7th, 2017.

CHAPTER 26

The Court of Claims' order

◆ ◆ ◆

THE JUDGE CHANGED THE DATE for review to 01/03/2018. I believed he moved the long date time ahead for making a discovery, so I started discovery. I filed 17 documents for admission and two interrogation requests to be answered. Once I filed discovery the Judge ignored the date of review and filed order granting defendants motion of disposition based on absolute quasi-judicial immunity. The claims for declaratory and injunctive relief could not be dismissed by any immunity. Prospective damage is similar to a case of a person wrongly imprisoned, he should be released once his status cleared but the Judge is immunized against the retroactive damages only.

The STATE OF MICHIGAN
COURT OF CLAIMS

Case No. 17-000229-MM Hon. Michael J. Talbot
ABDELBASET ABDELMAGID YOUSSEF, Plaintiff,
V.
DEPARTMENT OF LICENSING AND REGULATORY AFFAIRS, BUREAU OF PROFESSIONAL LICENSING, BOARD OF MEDICINE,

DENNIS SZYMANSKI, ROBERT REGAN, ANDREW HUDSON, JESSICA TAUB and JOHN HOPPER.

Defendants,

OPINION

Pending before the Court is defendants' motion for summary disposition, as well as plaintiff's motions for preliminary injunction, to strike defendants' reply brief, and to file a reply brief. The Court GRANTS plaintiff's motion to strike defendants' reply, and GRANTS plaintiff's motion to file a reply, thereby accepting plaintiff reply for filing. However, because the Court finds that defendants are entitled to immunity and because plaintiff's complaint is an improper attempt to re-litigate the suspension of his medical license, defendants' motion is GRANTED, and plaintiff's motion for preliminary injunction is DENIED as moot.

This matter arises out of the suspension of plaintiff's license to practice medicine. Plaintiff contested the suspension in a hearing before an administrative law judge (ALJ), who issued a proposal for final decision (PFD). On October 30, 2015, the Disciplinary Subcommittee for the Michigan Board of Medicine reviewed the PFD and adopted the findings and conclusions of law articulated therein. The Disciplinary Subcommittee suspended six months and one day, along with a $20,000 fine. Plaintiff appealed his suspension, and the Court of Appeals affirmed in an unpublished per curiam opinion. *In re Youssef,* unpublished opinion per curiam of the Court of Appeals, issued April 25, 2017 (Docket No. 330222). The Supreme Court denied leave to appeal on October 3, 2017. *In re Youssef,* Michigan (2017) (Docket No. 155701).

While his appeal was pending, plaintiff applied for reinstatement. An ALJ issued a PFD on the application for reinstatement on September 21, 2016, and recommended denying the application. The Board of Medicine adopted the PFD and extended plaintiff's suspension for a minimum of two years and one day. Plaintiff failed to timely appeal the denial of his application for reinstatement.

Although styled as an original action, plaintiff's complaint in the instant case is essentially a challenge to the suspension of his medical license. He asserts claims against the witnesses who testified at the hearing on his license suspension Robert Regan and Dr. John Hopper as well as a member of the Board of Medicine Dr. Dennis Szymanski and the two assistant attorneys general who prosecuted his license violation and opposed his application for reinstatement Andrew Hudson and Jessica Taub. In addition, he names as defendants the Department of Licensing and Regulatory Affairs, the Bureau of Professional Licensing, and the Board of Medicine.

Defendants have moved for summary disposition under MCR 2.116(C)(7), arguing that quasi-judicial immunity bars plaintiff's claims. "The doctrine of quasi-judicial immunity as developed by the common law" operates as a shield from liability.

The doctrine is a distinct concept from the legislative grant of immunity to judges in MCL 691.1407(5). The doctrine provides "absolute immunity" to those to whom it applies. *Serven* v *Health Quest Chiropractic, Inc.*, 319 Mich. App. 245, 249; 900 NW2d 671 (2017). It is, in essence, an extension of absolute judicial immunity to non-judicial officers *Id.* At 254 (citation omitted).

The Court agrees with defendants that the proceedings at issue, in this case, involved a quasi-judicial body. Indeed, "quasi-judicial immunity is frequently extended to a medical licensing board charged with hearing license suspension and revocation matters." *Id.* At 257. Recognizing as much, the Court of Appeals in *Serven* recently applied the doctrine in the context of a similar professional licensing board. See *id.* Seeing no reason to deviate from that approach based on the arguments made and pleadings submitted in the instant case, the Court concludes that the Board of Medicine, which acted through its Disciplinary Subcommittee, in this case, was a quasi-judicial body entitled to absolute immunity. This doctrine likewise applies to defendant Szymanski, whose only role, in this case, was serving as a member of the Board of Medicine.

Defendants Regan and Hopper are also entitled to immunity. Plaintiff's allegations against those defendants arise from their respective testimony at the hearing on the disciplinary complaint. It is well established that "witnesses who testify during the course of judicial proceedings enjoy quasi-judicial immunity." *Maiden* v *Rozwood,* 461 Mich 109, 134; 597 NW2d 817 (1999). "Witnesses who are an integral part of the judicial process are wholly immune from liability for the consequences of their testimony or related evaluations." *Id.* (quotation marks and citation omitted). A witness's statements made "during the course of judicial proceedings are absolutely privileged, provided they are relevant, material, or pertinent to the issue being tried." *Id.* The privilege is to be applied liberally, and "falsity or malice on the part of the witness does not abrogate the privilege." *Id.* Here, given the nature of the allegations against Regan and Hopper and the record evidence of their testimony, immunity applies to these defendants as well. This conclusion is unchanged by plaintiffs multiple contentions that both witnesses offered false testimony against him. See *id.* ("Falsity or malice on the part of the witness does not abrogate the privilege."). See also *Denhof,* 311 Mich. App at 520 (rejecting the notion that allegations of fraudulent misrepresentations by a witness can defeat the assertion of quasi-judicial immunity by a witness).

The two assistant attorneys general, Hudson, and Taub are entitled to quasi-judicial immunity as well. Indeed, the doctrine has been applied to those who function as assistant prosecuting attorneys in judicial proceedings. *Bischoff* v *Calhoun Co-Prosecutor,* 173 Michigan App 802, 808; 434 NW2d 249 (1988); *Payton* v *Wayne Co,* 137 Mich. App. 361, 371; 357 NW2d 700 (1984). The doctrine extends to bar civil suits "arising out of the initiation, prosecution, and presentment of the state's case." *Payton,* 173 Michigan App at 367, citing, *Imbler* v *Pachtman,* 424 US 409, 431; 96 S Ct 984; 47 L Ed 2d 128 (1976). Here, the allegations made against Hudson and Taub pertain to their respective actions in filing the disciplinary complaint, prosecuting the same by presenting witnesses and evidence and presenting the state's case in opposition to plaintiff's application for reinstatement of his license. Accordingly, the claims against Hudson and Taub must also be dismissed under the doctrine of quasi-judicial immunity.

To the extent plaintiff has asserted claims against the Bureau of Professional Licensing and the Department of Licensing and Regulatory Affairs that could survive the above conclusions, the Court concludes that those government agencies are entitled to immunity under MCL 691.1407(1). See also *Yoches v City of Dearborn,* Michigan App. NW2d

(2017); slip op at 10 (stating that the unambiguous language of MCL 691.1407(1) provides immunity to governmental agencies).

As an alternative, the Court concludes that to the extent, the plaintiff is attempting to challenge the suspension of his license or the subsequent denial of his application for reinstatement, such challenges constitute an impermissible collateral attack. "It is well established in Michigan that, assuming competent jurisdiction, a party cannot use the second proceeding to attack a tribunal's decision in a previous proceeding" *Workers' Compensation*

Agency Dir. V MacDonald's Indus Prod, Inc., 305 Mich. App. 460, 474; 853 NW2d 467 (2014).

Plaintiff cannot, in this collateral proceeding, attack the underlying decision to suspend his license or to deny his application for reinstatement.

Date October 18, 2017, Michael Talbot, Judge

CHAPTER 27

The Court denied relief for unknown cause

◆ ◆ ◆

THE JUDGE DISMISSED THE COMPLAINT about absolute quasi-judicial immunity shields the defendants. The absolute quasi-judicial immunity shields the defendants from the retrospective claims such as compensation for damage but does not immunize the prospective violations. Example if a person was wrongly imprisoned he could not sue the judge for the past damage however he should be released once the status was cleared that the order was wrong. The Judge scheduled review on 1/3/2018, but once I started discovery and I filed 17 documents to the defendants for admission and two interrogation requests, the judge granted the defendants' motion to dismiss based on absolute quasi-judicial immunity, but he did not address the injunctive relief that means reinstatement of the license. The quasi-judicial immunity did not immunize the defendants against correction of the ongoing wrong.

Injunction required discovery and the defendants were trying to avoid discovery anyway, so I filed this motion and suggested offer that the defendants could save themselves from discovery by just reinstating my license. The Judge denied this motion without explanations. I did not file an appeal, because the appeal takes years and give nothing but further retaliation, in the same time the Judge who issued the order in the Court of Claims, he the Chief Judge of Michigan Court of Appeals.

Next is my motion. I requested the Judge my address the prospective injunctive relief and permitted discovery. The defendants could be saved from discovery by just reinstatement my license.

THE STATE OF MICHIGAN
MICHIGAN COURT OF CLAIMS
925 W. Ottawa St
P. O. Box 30185, Lansing, MI, 48909

Docket No. 17-000229-MM Honorable: Michael Talbot
Abdelbaset Youssef, Pro Se.
Plaintiff

Vs.

Department of Licensing and Regulatory Affairs (LARA). Et al.
Defendants

10/23/2017, PLAINTIFF'S MOTION FOR RELIEF FROM JUDGMENT MCR 2.612(C)(1)(f) AND MCR 2.605

I, Pro Se plaintiff, Abdelbaset Youssef, herby move the honorable court of claims may grant me motion for relief from judgment was entered on October 18, 2017, MCR 2.612(C)(1)(f). The court may permit completing discovery for pending trial of the Declaratory and prospective Injunctive relief claims.

The Court granted defendants motion for summary disposition based only on quasi-judicial immunity. Declaratory and prospective injunction claims were not addressed in the order, and the discovery is still pending. Quasi-judicial Immunity alone does not immunize defendants from declaratory relief and prospective injunction of documented continuous violations of the constitutional rights.

Defendants do not claim that my case does not state claim upon which relief could be granted MCR 2.116(C)(8), and discovery is still pending.

Defendants do not deny claims that suspension of license six months was issued without due process in retaliation for I did not accept paying $5000 fine and the PFD that recommended denying reinstatement was clearly and openly stated that it was retaliation for filing an appeal and based on intentionally prepared the false document and perjury under oath. *"I do not know what pending retaliation will be for filing this complaint in this court!"*

I cannot get a license in another state because my license in Michigan is suspended. Defendants are trying to use immunity to make the Constitutions functionless papers and the state officials above any civil Law.

AFFIDAVIT UNDER OATH AND BRIEF

I - Statement of facts

1. On 8/16/2017, I filed this complaint about constitutional questions, claimed declaratory and injunctive reliefs and compensatory and punitive reliefs.

2. On 9/7/2017, I filed a motion for preliminary injunction.

3. On 9/15/2017, defendants filed a motion for summary disposition based on quasi-judicial immunity.

4. On 10/6/2017, plaintiff sent email to the defendants' attorney he told him that the Honorable Judge Talbot had moved the date of reviewing the case to 1/3/2018 to give time for discovery and he requested them to start discovery.

5. On 10/16/2017, plaintiff filed first discovery request included 17 documents for admission and two interrogatory requests.

6. On 10/18/2017, Honorable Judge Talbot filed order granted defendants' motion for summary disposition.

II - Argument

A. Federal Courts do not allow defendants defeat declaratory and prospective injunctive relief by immunity

A. The defendants are trying to dismiss my claims for declaratory and injunctive reliefs through a motion to dismiss based only on the governmental and quasi-judicial immunity. Immunity could not defeat declaratory and prospective injunction. Even the Eleventh Amendment does not immune state from the injunction of continuous violations.

B. Courts Judicial Immunity Prospective relief and attorney's fees allowed.

Pulliam v. Allen, 104 S. Ct. 1970 (1984). On January 10, 1980, the police arrested Richmond Allen in Culpepper Co., Virginia for using abusive language. The offense was a misdemeanor for which there was no jail sentence; the maximum penalty was a $500.00 fine. Magistrate Pulliam set bail at $250.00, and when Allen was unable to meet it, she committed him to jail until his trial fourteen days later. After his release and payment of the fine, Allen brought a section 1983 action against Magistrate Pulliam and Judge Burke, before whom he had been tried, seeking declaratory and injunctive relief. The United States District Court for the Eastern District of Virginia found the practice of incarcerating persons for non-incarcerable offenses to be a violation of due process and equal protection and prospectively enjoined Magistrate Pulliam. Pursuant to section 1988, Allen was granted his request of $7,038 in attorney's fees and the award was upheld by the

Fourth Circuit Court of Appeals. The Supreme Court granted certiorari and held that judicial immunity does not bar prospective injunctive relief under section 1983 of the Civil Rights Act of 18715 or bar the award of attorney's fees under the Civil Rights Attorney's Fees Award.

B. Michigan Governmental Immunity act immunizes state agencies, officers, and judges from tort claims only but it is not for a prospective injunction.

A. Defendants do not claim the wrongs, and the violations did not happen but instead, they rely on immunity as escape windows. Theoretically, if we consider them immune, the immunity is for retroactive tort claims only, it will not be extended to cover their prospective violations for good.

B. MCL691.1407(5) (5) A judge, a legislator, and the elective or highest appointive executive official of all levels of government are immune from tort liability for injuries to persons or damages to property if he or she is acting within the scope of his or her judicial, legislative, or executive authority.

III– Declaratory judgment is available to the plaintiff:

MCR 2.605 DECLARATORY JUDGMENTS

(A) Power to Enter Declaratory Judgment.

(1) In a case of actual controversy within its jurisdiction, a Michigan court of record may declare the rights and other legal relations of an interested party seeking a declaratory judgment, whether or not another relief is or could be sought or granted.

(2) For the purpose of this rule, an action is considered within the jurisdiction of a court if the court would have jurisdiction of an action on the same

claim or claims in which the plaintiff sought relief other than a declaratory judgment.

(B) Procedure. The procedure for obtaining declaratory relief is in accordance with these rules, and the right to trial by jury may be demanded under the circumstances and in the manner provided in the constitution, statutes, and court rules of the State of Michigan.

(C) Other Adequate Remedy. The existence of another adequate remedy does not preclude a judgment for declaratory relief in an appropriate case.

(D) Hearing. The court may order a speedy hearing of an action for declaratory relief and may advance it on the calendar.

(E) Effect; Review. Declaratory judgments have the force and effect of and are reviewable as, final judgments.

(F) Other Relief. Further necessary or proper relief based on a declaratory judgment may be granted, after reasonable notice and hearing, against a party whose rights have been determined by the declaratory judgment.

IV - Conclusion and requested reliefs

1. The Court had decided that: due to the quasi-judicial immunity of defendants, I have to lose my rights of compensations for the damages.

2. It is not hard for the Board of Medicine and the Attorney General that they may break the vicious circle of the escalated retaliations and reinstate my medical license to let me survive the remaining short part of my life.

3. I pray the honorable judge may permit completing the discovery for pending trial the declaratory and permanent prospective injunction claims and any further order may see it properly.

4. Defendants may avoid the discovery, and the declaratory and prospective injunctive relief judgments by settlement lead to reinstating my license clean without any restrictions on its condition that was before 10/30/2015.

Respectfully submitted

By __________ Pro Se Plaintiff, Abdelbaset Youssef, 10/23/201

Made in the USA
Monee, IL
04 November 2026

67382719R00154